History of the Vikings

A Captivating Guide to the Viking Age and Feared Norse Seafarers Such as Ragnar Lothbrok, Ivar the Boneless, Egil Skallagrimsson, and More

Free Bonus from Captivating History (Available for a Limited time)

Hi History Lovers!

Now you have a chance to join our exclusive history list so you can get your first history ebook for free as well as discounts and a potential to get more history books for free! Simply visit the link below to join.

Captivatinghistory.com/ebook

Also, make sure to follow us on:

Twitter: @Captivhistory

Facebook: Captivating History:@captivatinghistory

Contents

Introduction

The predominant modern image of the mighty Viking warriors has become that of the warmonger and marauding berserker. In popular culture, the Norsemen, portrayed as giant, sword-wielding men with flowing hair and bushy beards, have been reduced to a one-dimensional tribe of ruthless warriors, who cared little for the communities they attacked and plundered. Men like Ragnar Lothbrok, Eric Bloodaxe, Ivar the Boneless and Bjorn Ironside are portrayed as preying on unsuspecting communities and spreading fear across Europe as they laid waste to all that lay before them, taking what they wanted at the point of a sword. It is true that the Vikings were, without a doubt, brutal men living in a brutal age. They did use their skills as warriors to relentlessly attack Europe and the British Isles to increase their wealth and territory, but that is not all the Vikings were, and their contribution to world history is far more than warmongering.

Juxtaposed to the fearless warrior image is a less ruthless version of the Vikings and their place in history. It is the story of ordinary men and women who carved out a living on the harsh and unforgiving shores of the icy North Sea. It is also the story of extraordinary men, like Erik the Red and, his son, Leif Erikson who were great explorers, master seafarers, and brave colonizers. Men who were not just heroic warriors but were also not afraid to sail across the vast ocean in open longboats to search for new lands and unclaimed territories. Men who changed the face of the world they were born into as they discovered new continents, spreading their culture far and wide. It is important to realize that these two images of the Vikings are not mutually exclusive. It's not one or the other, but both.

The Vikings were farmers, traders, and craftsmen who raided and plundered when it suited their needs or when they were not busy working their lands. They were part of a structured and organized society, who believed in fairness and justice, and were governed by the rule of law. They were family men who enjoyed feasting, poetry, and board games, and took part in competitions that tested their strength and military prowess. And yes, they were also brutal warriors. They fought amongst themselves to increase their individual wealth and consolidate their power as they defined the borders of Scandinavia that we recognize today. They ruthlessly attacked and plundered the British Isles again and again. But they also settled there and had a significant influence on British culture, and some even became kings of England. They were great military strategists, who would just as easily sign a peace treaty as go to war. The Vikings were a complex society that contributed greatly to world history.

The Viking Age, which lasted from circa 790 CE to 1066 CE, was a time of great conquest, expansion, and exploration for the Scandinavian countries. As such, theirs is a history of raiders and plunders, but it is also a history of settlers and explorers. The men, and the myths, that the Viking Age gave rise to offer historians great insight into world history, as well as Norse culture and society, and their stories have kept the legend of the Vikings alive for centuries.

Section One: An Overview of the Viking Age

Chapter One: The Rise of the Mighty Vikings and the Viking Age (Circa 790 CE to 1066 CE)

The period from the earliest recorded raids in the 790s until the Norman Conquest of England in 1066 is commonly known as the Viking Age of Scandinavian history. For 300 years, beginning at the end of the 8th century, Scandinavians figure prominently in the history of Western Europe, first as pirates and later as conquerors and colonists.[1]

Throughout history, the world has seen the rise and fall of many empires. Some, like the Romans and the British, have left an indelible mark on history and are remembered for their great accomplishments, while others have faded into relative obscurity. Regardless of how empires, and their rulers, are judged by history, it is important to remember that all have changed the face of the world around them. And in that regard, the Vikings are similar to many of the great empires the world has seen. However, the Vikings were not empire builders in the true sense of the word. Nor did they build a Viking Empire that fits into the traditional model, but they did colonize and conquer vast lands and leave their mark on history.

One aspect of the Vikings that makes them different from traditional empires is that the Vikings did not originate from one country and had no national identity. They had no central government or single monarch, nor were they a unified group who attacked other countries to expand their national influence and territories. The Vikings were smaller groups of warriors, who in the early years of the Viking Age attacked vulnerable settlements to increase their personal wealth and prestige. They raided and plundered communities in hit-and-run attacks before returning to their homelands. In later years they did rule parts of the British Isles, but they never sought to build a cohesive Norse empire.

It is important to recognize that the Vikings were definitely not a distinct race or tribe. During the Viking Age, the term Viking was applied to all the raiders who came from the northern territories and attacked villages and monasteries in Europe and the British Isles. What differentiated the Norsemen from the communities that they attacked was their foreignness, and more importantly the fact that they were pagans and not Christians.

The Vikings came from the area that is now known as Scandinavia, and included Denmark, Finland, Sweden, Norway, as well as Iceland and Greenland. But these were not the modern nations we know today with distinct national identities, but rather an assortment of settlements, communities, and kingdoms. They may not have been a nation, but these northern men, or Norsemen, shared a common socio-cultural distinctiveness from the rest of Europe. They were bound by a shared history and common traits of culture, one of them being the kinship of native languages.[2]

Since the Vikings were not a single nation but rather a group of kingdoms and settlements on the Scandinavian Peninsula, their history is also not one cohesive story. Viking history is fragmented and at times confusing, and because it is the history of a loosely associated group held together by their cultural similarities, it does not follow a linear progression or storyline. This lack of cohesion is further compounded by the fact that the Vikings had no written history.

Much of what we know of the Vikings is based on the sagas and chronicles written in later centuries. These are very informative works and important historical resources, but it is important to remember that they were also written to serve a political or religious agenda, and this has, at times, led to an obscuring of facts and a proliferation of myths and legends. Battles have been exaggerated, and mere mortals turned into legendary warriors. That is not to say the accounts should be dismissed as pure works of fiction; they are merely embellished versions of historical events that did, for the most part, actually take place.

Many of the stories and legends of the Vikings contain similar information and consistent facts. It is well known that for many centuries, the Norsemen were content in their various homelands. There they raised their families, tended their livestock, and worked the land. But like many societies, there came a time when they were no longer satisfied to remain in the lands of their birth and began to venture farther afield.

Like most things in history, there is not one reason, or single occurrence, that gave rise to the Viking Age, but rather a combination of circumstances and events. There are many reasons why the Norsemen may have left their homes and began raiding and plundering European communities. The most common explanation for the rise of the Viking Age is the pursuit of wealth. During the 8th century, the European nations were becoming wealthier, and the Vikings saw an opportunity to share in Europe's rising fortunes. There is no doubt that the pursuit of wealth was a driving force behind the Viking Age.

But it was not the only reason. Some of the other theories that have been put forward as causes of the Viking Age are population pressure, primogeniture, the rise of Christianity and its effect on trade, power struggles and the consolidation of kingdoms, and an abundance of vulnerable targets. These are all valid assumptions, but on closer inspection, some make more sense than others.

Most historians today agree that population pressure did not have a large influence on the Viking Age. But it may have played a supporting role, especially when considered in conjunction with primogeniture. Primogeniture meant that the oldest son inherited everything and the younger sons had to make their own fortunes. Without access to farmland, the younger sons had to look elsewhere to support themselves. To them, raiding would have been an appealing option. It was a way to substantially increase their wealth and standing in their communities.

The rise of Christianity could also have influenced the Norsemen and their need to expand their territories. For centuries, the Scandinavians had traded throughout Europe, but as the European nations converted to Christianity, they became less and less inclined to trade with pagans. This decline in trade, and therefore wealth, may have led the Vikings to resolve the situation through raids. The fact that the Vikings were not Christian also meant that they had no qualms about attacking wealthy, religious institutions in Europe. Churches and monasteries were not well protected because Christians did not attack their own religious houses, and the Vikings would have seen them as soft targets.

During the Viking Age, it was not just Europe and the British Isles that were under threat from these ruthless warriors. The Norsemen often waged war against each other, and as some of the stronger rulers began to consolidate their power, weaker chiefs were forced into exile. But it was not only ousted chiefs who rejected the rule of unpopular monarchs. Many regular citizens also left their homelands to avoid living under the control of a ruthless king. For example, during the rule of Harald Fairhair many Norwegians left their homeland and settled in Iceland.

As the Vikings were either forced from their homelands or began exploring the wider world out of curiosity, they were exposed to Europe's growing wealth, and they recognized an opportunity to increase their own wealth and power. They realized that they were superior warriors and that many of Europe's coastal monasteries were easy targets.

The first recorded raid by the Vikings was an attack on the undefended coastal monastery of Lindisfarne on the British Isles in 793 CE. This is regarded as the start of the Viking Age, a terrifying time for the unprotected communities along the coast of Europe and the British Isles. The Vikings soon became relentless in their attacks, and when they were not farming, they were plundering. This pattern went on for centuries, and shaped the history of Europe and more noticeably the British Isles.

These early raids gave the Vikings their first taste of European wealth, and once they realized how lucrative raiding was, they crossed the treacherous oceans and high seas in all directions to plunder and terrorize settlements up and down the coast of the British Isles, France, Italy, and Russia. Due to their well-designed and shallow-hulled longboats, they were also able to travel up rivers and raid communities farther inland. No one was safe from these fearsome Norsemen, and soon the Vikings reputation preceded them. The mere sight of a longboat sailing upriver was enough to strike terror in the hearts of any European community and many fled before them.

[1]Peter Sawyer, *The Viking Expansion*, The Cambridge History of Scandinavia, Issue 1 (Knut Helle, ed., 2003), p. 105

[2]The Cambridge History of Scandinavia, Issue 1 (Knut Helle, ed., 2003), p. 4

Chapter Two: A Timeline and Overview of Significant Viking Raids and Battles

The early raids on the coastal monasteries of the British Isles were merely the opening salvos in a series of attacks and battles that lasted for centuries. An overview of the Vikings significant raids and battles provides insight into their history and culture. Not only did the Vikings plunder up and down the coast of Europe amassing great riches, but they also fought amongst themselves as they strove to consolidate power in their own homelands. These battles demonstrate that the Norsemen were not averse to violence and the use of force to achieve their goals.

All the battles that the Vikings were involved in over the centuries are far too numerous to mention. There are, however, some that stand out for their ruthlessness or the impact they had on world history. A brief look at these battles also provides a basic timeline for Viking history.

793 – Viking raid on Lindisfarne

The raid on Lindisfarne in 793 was significant because it marked the beginning of the Viking Age. The attack was unexpected and brutal, but what truly shocked the British and their European neighbors was that these new invaders had no respect for religious institutions.

795 – First Viking raids on the European continent

In 795, the Vikings launched their next raid on the British Isles, and plundered the undefended monasteries on Skye and Iona in the Hebrides, as well as Rathlin off the northeast coast of Ireland. From there they turned their focus towards the continent itself, and the first raid on mainland Europe was an attack on the island monastery of St Philibert's on Noirmautier. From then on, the Vikings used their shallow-hulled longboats to sail along the coast of Europe and up rivers to launch swift hit-and-run raids on unsuspecting and undefended settlements. These early attacks were quick, efficient, and decisive. The Vikings landed, attacked, took what they wanted, including slaves, and retreated before the communities had time to defend themselves or launch counterattacks.

845 – Ragnar Lothbrok's raid on Paris

In 845, Ragnar Lothbrok sailed up the river Seine and launched a brutal and decisive attack on Paris. He sacked the city and then held it for ransom until King Charles the Bald agreed to pay him 7,000 French livres. This was a significant Viking attack because it demonstrated that not even the inland European towns and cities were safe from the mighty Vikings. It also showed that the Vikings were not interested in colonization at that time. Once King Charles had paid the ransom, the Vikings left Paris and returned to their homeland.

860 – Bjorn Ironside raids the Mediterranean

According to legend, Ragnar was the founder of a great Viking dynasty, and his sons were just as ruthless as their father and did their own fair share of raiding. His son, Bjorn Ironside, sailed his longboats along the coast of Spain and through the Straits of Gibraltar in 860 to plunder towns on the shores of the Mediterranean.

865 – The Great Heathen Army attacks England

In 865, Bjorn joined his brother, Ivar the Boneless, and attacked England to avenge the death of their father at the hands of King Aella of Northumbria. By then, the British Isles had been raided many times, but this was the first time that a Viking army, known as the Great Heathen Army, came to conquer the British kingdoms. The English were wholly unprepared for the mighty force that landed on their shores, and this attack was the death knell for the Kingdom of Northumbria.

872 – Battle of Hafrsfjord

The Norsemen did not, however, confine their battles to foreign shores. Harald Fairhair spent ten years fighting against his neighboring kingdoms on the Norwegian Peninsula. After much bloodshed, his campaign culminated in the epic Battle of Hafrsfjord in 872. He was finally able to defeat the last of his enemies, and consolidated his power to become the first king of Norway. Harald's victory was significant in Norwegian history, because after the battle, western Norway was united under one king for the first time.

878 – Battle of Edington

In the years that followed the 865 attack on Northumbria, the Vikings spread throughout Anglo-Saxon England. Their advance was finally halted by Alfred the Great, king of Wessex, in 878. During early clashes between the Vikings and King Alfred, it seemed as though Alfred would suffer the same fate as most of his compatriots. His army was decimated on the battlefield, and he was driven out of his own country. But unlike so many others, Alfred the Great refused to admit defeat, and he gathered an army of local men to face the Vikings at the Battle of Edington. This was a resounding victory for the English, and it secured Alfred a place in history as one of the great English monarchs.

999 – Battle of Svolder

The Battle of Svolder, circa 999, took place between King Olaf Tryggvason of Norway and an alliance between King Sweyn Forkbeard of Denmark and King Olaf Skotkonung of Sweden. The battle was fought at sea, and was an unfair fight between ten Norwegian ships and approximately 70 Danish and Swedish vessels. King Olaf Tryggvason was killed in battle, and Norway then fell under the rule of the Kingdom of Denmark.

1014 – Battle of Clontarf

The Vikings are remembered as great and accomplished warriors, but they were not always successful on the battlefield. They also suffered their fair share of defeats. The Battle of Clontarf (near modern-day Dublin) was one such devastating loss, and it marked a turning point in medieval Irish history. The battle took place on April 23, 1014 between the Irish king, Brian Boru, and a Norse-Irish alliance led by Sigtrygg Silkbeard, king of Dublin. The defeat of the Norse forces effectively ended the Viking domination of Ireland.

1016 - Battle of Assandun

This was a significant clash because it led to the establishment of a short-lived line of Viking kings in England. The battle was fought between the forces of Edmond Ironside, newly crowned king of England and the son of Aethelred the Unready, and the legendary Cnut the Great. Even though the battle ended in a decisive victory for Cnut, the two men decided to divide England between them. However, Edmond died only a few short weeks later, and Cnut became king of England. He and his sons ruled the country for the next 26 years.

1066 – Battle of Fulford

The Battle of Fulford was part of a series of clashes that proved significant in British history and culminated in the famous Battle of Hastings. At Fulford, the English could have faced the Vikings from behind the walls of York, but they chose to come out and fight on the battlefield. This was a devastating military blunder. The English crossed the Ouse River in an attempt to break the Viking "shield wall," but they were unsuccessful and this led to a decisive Viking victory.

1066 – Battle of Stamford Bridge and Battle of Hastings

The next major battle was the Battle of Stamford Bridge, and this is regarded as the last great battle of the Viking Age on English soil. The battle took place near York in September 1066 and was fought between King Harald Godwinson of England and King Harald Hardrada of Norway. It was a decisive victory for the English, with King Harald Hardrada dying on the battlefield. The battle may have been an English victory, but it still had devastating consequences for the nation of England. The Battle of Hastings, fought between William the Conqueror and King Harald Godwinson, followed soon after the Battle of Stamford Bridge, and it is one of the most significant turning points in British history. Although it was not fought between the English and Vikings, the Norsemen played a role in the outcome. The battle-weary Englishmen, who had been weakened by their clash with King Hardrada, were no match for the French, and this gave William the Conqueror, duke of Normandy, the edge he needed to defeat the English and claim the crown.

Section Two: Heroes and Villains

The Viking Age was a time of great expansion for the Scandinavian nations, and their influence could be felt far and wide. During this time, thousands of Norsemen and women left their homelands to conquer, colonize, raid, and plunder. Some even uprooted their families to start new lives elsewhere. The Swedes predominantly went east to Russia and the surrounding areas, while the Danes explored the North Sea coastline, England, and France. The Norwegians crossed the North Sea to the British Isles and the Norwegian Sea, eventually ending up on the shores of Iceland and Greenland.

As a whole, the names of most of the Viking warriors and adventurers were never recorded, and their identities have long since faded into obscurity. Fortunately, the Viking Age did produce some interesting characters whose names have survived and whose legends have grown with time. Men, mostly jarls and royalty, who left an enduring mark on world history and kept the legend of the Viking warrior alive in popular culture and modern imagination.

The image of the mighty Viking has been built on the backs of legendary men like Ragnar Lothbrok, Ivar the Boneless, Bjorn Ironside, Egil Skallagrimsson, Harald Fairhair, Eric Bloodaxe, Sweyn Forkbeard, Harald Hardrada, Erik the Red, and Leif Eriksson, to name but a few. Depending on what side of their swords you found yourself on, they were either great heroes or terrifying villains. But regardless of how they have been judged by history, they have certainly not been forgotten. By looking at these individuals, their exploits, and the way they are remembered, scholars have been able to build a much clearer picture of Viking history and ideals.

Chapter Three: Ragnar Lothbrok – Man or Myth

Ragnar Lothbrok is one of those historical characters, like King Arthur in Britain, which historians cannot reach a consensus about. They don't seem to be able to agree as to whether he actually existed or not. Is he one man, whose legend has grown and been embellished over centuries until the myth no longer resembles reality? Is he an amalgamation of different historical characters, or is he simply the figment of a cultural imagination? The truth is historians just don't know. There are no surviving records from this time, and most information is based on the sagas and historical chronicles that were written in later centuries, by historians with their own political and religious agendas. But regardless of whether Ragnar really existed or not, he has become the embodiment of the legendary Viking warrior.

Those who believe that Ragnar Lothbrok was one man describe him as a Viking warlord and hero, who lived during the 9th century and was the son of the Danish King Sigurd Ring. The *Anglo-Saxon Chronicle* gives a good account of Ragnar (Lothbrok) Sigurdsson and his exploits that had a significant impact on Britain and France in the 9th century. According to legend, he made his fortune by ruthlessly attacking and plundering English and French villages, and was even rumored to have attacked people while they were praying in their churches. Ragnar Lothbrok was clearly a man without mercy or religious sentiments.

He was the scourge of both England and France as he raided the Anglian kingdoms of Northumbria and Wessex, along with the Kingdom of West Francia, on many occasions. He used the rivers of Europe and the shallow hulls of his longboats to his advantage and sailed far inland. He even attacked Paris in 845. During this raid, his forces were so ruthless that they destroyed an entire division of King Charles the Bald's army. He only withdrew from the city after receiving a ransom payment of 7,000 French livres.

It is important to note that Lothbrok was not his surname but rather his nickname, which meant "hairy or dirty pants." There is no clear explanation as to how he came by this nickname. According to *Ragnar's Saga* (written in the 13th century), it was because of the pants he wore to protect himself when he fought a poison-breathing serpent or dragon. Another, less flattering theory is that when he was dying of dysentery, he soiled his pants. But if historians cannot even agree on whether or not the man existed, it is doubtful that the true story behind his nickname will ever be revealed.

Ragnar reputedly married three or four times and had a host of children. He is famous not only for his own exploits on the battlefield, but also for being the father of a ruthless and violent dynasty. His sons included Ivar the Boneless, Sigurd Snake-in-the-eye, and Bjorn Ironside, who were all famous warriors and significant historical figures in their own right. They fought alongside their father and on their own, and became the bane of Europe. They raided settlements in Russia, the Baltics, the Mediterranean, and numerous other territories, but France and England were their main targets.

Even the death of Ragnar is disputed. One version is not very heroic and claims that he died of disease, quite possibly dysentery, shortly after he sacked Paris. The other version of his death is far more gruesome and painful. According to legend, Ragnar was returning home after his attack on Paris when his ship was blown off course and ran aground on English soil. He was captured by Aella, the king of Northumbria, and in revenge for Ragnar's numerous attacks on his kingdom, he threw Ragnar into a pit of vipers where he met a grisly end. Although he did not realize it at the time, by killing Ragnar King Aella had made an enemy of perhaps the most dangerous man of the 9th century, Ragnar's son Ivar the Boneless.

Shortly before he died, Ragnar is rumored to have said that his sons would avenge his death. This did, in due course, come to pass, and a horde of Vikings, led by Ragnar's sons and known as the Great Heathen Army, invaded England in 865 and killed King Aella. By killing Ragnar, the Northumbrian king had doomed his own kingdom and changed the course of English history.

Chapter Four: Ivar the Boneless – Ruthless Warrior, Leader of the Great Heathen Army, and Conqueror of England

Ivar the Boneless[1] was the son of Ragnar Lothbrok and his second wife Aslaug. There is no historical record of where his moniker originated; therefore, it is open to interpretation and speculation, and it is not all complimentary. One theory suggests that since Ivar never married or had children, he was impotent, hence the unflattering nickname. Another, and perhaps more likely, version is that he was a cripple who suffered from some kind of genetic defect. It has been suggested by historians that this could have been Osteogenesis Imperfecta, a rare, genetic condition that can result in bone deformities and fractures. Another explanation is Ehlers-Danlos syndrome, which is a group of genetic connective tissue disorders that cause recurrent joint dislocations and joint hypermobility. In the *Ragnar's Saga*, Ivar is born with deformed legs because of a curse.

There is another, more flattering theory that says the name refers to his speed and agility in battle. Since there is no historical record that accurately describes Ivar's condition, all these theories are based on speculation and it remains unclear as to how Ivar Ragnarsson became Ivar the Boneless. But interesting as it is to speculate on the origins of his nickname, it is an aside to the story of this mighty Viking's deeds.

What historians do appear to agree on is that Ivar was a fearsome warrior, cunning leader, and brutal warlord. But he was more than just a marauding Viking, picking on soft targets he was also a great leader of men and military strategist.

In 865, a large Viking force, led by Ivar the Boneless and known as the Great Heathen Army, descended upon the Anglo-Saxon Heptarchy.[2] As Ragnar had predicted, his sons had come to avenge his death. But this great Viking army was different from anything that the English had experienced before. For the first time in history, a Viking force had come not to plunder, but arrived with the intent of occupying the British Isles. The English were accustomed to attacks by raiding parties but never before had these parties come to conquer the English kingdoms, and the English were wholly unprepared for the invaders that landed on their shores. Ivar's brief rule in England was one of brutality and vengeance, as the Vikings had no qualms about inflicting great cruelty on the local population. At the time the Great Heathen Army invaded England, King Aella of Northumbria was involved in a civil war. King Osberht, whose throne he usurped But when the Vikings reached York, King Aella and King Osberht realized that they had to put aside their differences and unite against their common enemy if they wanted to survive. Unfortunately, they were no match for Ivar the Boneless and his warriors. The English tried to stand their ground, but they were slaughtered in battle. King Osberht died on the battlefield, and King Aella was taken prisoner.

Ivar the Boneless and his brothers showed King Aella no mercy, and he was ruthlessly executed as revenge for killing their father. Some historians suggest that Ivar the Boneless tortured and killed King Aella by means of the Blood Eagle.[3] The defeat of the English and the death of King Aella marked the end of the Kingdom of Northumbria as an independent entity.

Ivar the Boneless then led his army into the heart of Saxon England, but by now the English had realized that if they didn't present a united front, their kingdoms would be destroyed one by one. Wessex and Mercia joined forces against the Vikings. But Ivar, being a good military strategist, knew when to fight and when to negotiate. When his army was besieged at Nottingham, he negotiated for peace and returned to York. Henry of Huntingdon, writing almost 250 years after Ivar's death, described the situation as such, "Ingwar [Ivar] then, seeing that the whole force of England was there gathered, and that his host was the weaker, and was there shut in, betook himself to smooth words—cunning fox that he was—and won peace and troth from the English. Then he went back to York, and abode there one year with all cruelty."[4]

But peace did not last long. The Vikings returned to East Anglia, and when King Edmund led an army against them, he was captured and brutally executed. He was first beaten with clubs, then tied to a tree and shot with arrows. His body was beheaded, and his head was thrown into a bramble bush. After killing King Edmund of East Anglia, Ivar continued his rampage, moving north and plundering parts of Scotland before settling in Dublin. Shortly after that, Ivar the Boneless disappears from historical records, and it is thought that he died peacefully in Dublin sometime in the 870s. Ivar the Boneless was without a doubt a great military leader and a ruthless Viking warrior. He was responsible for the death of three kings, but he also united three English kingdoms into the Norse state of Danelaw (the northern, eastern, and central parts of Anglo-Saxon England in which Danish law and customs were observed), thereby changing both the course of British and Norse history. Before the Great Heathen Army attacked England, the Vikings were raiders and plunderers whose greatest accomplishment had been the sacking of Paris, but thanks to the exploits of Ivar the Boneless, they had become conquerors and colonizers who retained a foothold in the British Isles until 1066.

[1] *As with Ragnar Lothbrok, there is some confusion over the true identity of Ivar the Boneless. He may have been one man, but he could also be an amalgamation of various Viking warriors. There are numerous mentions of an Ivar, Ingwar, and Imar in Viking history but it is unclear as to whether these all refer to the same man. The Annals of Ireland and the Annals of Ulster record the death of Imar in*

873. Many historians believe that this is Ivar the Boneless. If one accepts that Ragnar Lothbrok was one man, then Ivar was his son.

[2] *The Heptarchy is a collective name applied to the seven petty kingdoms of Anglo-Saxon England from the Anglo-Saxon settlement of Britain in the 5th century until their unification into the Kingdom of England in the early 10th century. The term "Heptarchy" alludes to the tradition that there were seven Anglo-Saxon kingdoms, usually enumerated as: East Anglia, Essex, Kent, Mercia, Northumbria, Sussex, and Wessex. The Anglo-Saxon kingdoms eventually unified into the Kingdom of England.*

(https://en.wikipedia.org/wiki/Heptarchy)

[3] *The Blood Eagle is one of the most graphic, cruel, and slow torture methods ever described, and it's associated with the Vikings. According to 12th- and 13th-century authors, the Blood Eagle had a long tradition in Scandinavia and was used against their most heinous enemies. The conventional interpretation of the Viking Blood Eagle is that it was done by carving an eagle onto the back of one's enemy, prying his back open by detaching his ribs from his backbone, and pulling his lungs through the opening. The lungs were then spread over the ribs, giving the impression of wings. This made the body look like a spread eagle, albeit a mutilated one.*

(Lassie Smith, Details about the Blood Eagle, One of History's Most Nightmarish Torture Methods, Weird History)

[4] http://www.englishmonarchs.co.uk/vikings_10.html

Chapter Five: Bjorn Ironside – Raider of the Mediterranean

Bjorn Ironside was a typical Viking and many of his exploits are recorded in the *Saga of King Heidrek the Wise* and the *Saga of Ragnar's Sons*, as well as other early medieval writings. He was the oldest son of Ragnar Lothbrok and his second wife Aslaug, and the brother of Ivar the Boneless and Sigurd Snake-in-the-eye. When Ragnar Lothbrok died, Scandinavia was split between Bjorn and a number of his brothers. Bjorn became the king of Sweden and was the founder of the House of Munsö, a dynasty that went on to rule Sweden for several generations.

Like his father Ragnar Lothbrok and his brother Ivar the Boneless, Bjorn Ironside was renowned during the Viking Age for his raids on France. He fought alongside his famous father and he successfully raided up and down the coast of France, but he is most famous for his impressive raids in the Mediterranean. Having heard that there were many riches to plunder on the Mediterranean coast, Bjorn Ironside, along with his loyal friend and mentor, Hastein, attacked settlements on the Spanish coast all the way down to Gibraltar before leading his large raiding party into the Mediterranean in 860.

Bjorn Ironside sailed through the Straits of Gibraltar to plunder the south of France and Italy. After capturing Pisa, Bjorn turned his sights on Rome. He had heard stories of the vast wealth that had been amassed by the city that lay at the very heart of Christendom. Unfortunately, Bjorn's sense of direction was not that good, and instead of laying siege to Rome, he mistakenly besieged the town of Luna. Unlike so many other towns, Luna did not immediately fall to his sword, and to avoid a long and drawn-out engagement, Bjorn was forced to resort to trickery to breach the town walls.

In one version of the story, Hastein sent word to the bishop of Luna that Bjorn had died but that he had converted to Christianity on his deathbed and wanted to be buried in consecrated ground. In another version, Hastein sent word to the bishop that Bjorn was desperately ill and wanted to convert to Christianity before he died. Regardless of which story is more accurate, the bishop allowed Bjorn to be bought into the city. He was carried into the church by an honor guard before leaping to his feet, sword in hand, and leading his men as they fought their way to the town gate and let in the rest of their army to sack Luna.

After their victory in Luna, Bjorn and his men raided towns in Sicily and North Africa. But, like his father, Bjorn was not a colonizer, and once he had done enough raiding in the Mediterranean, he decided to return to Sweden. But getting out of the Mediterranean was going to prove slightly trickier than Bjorn had anticipated. By the time he reached the Straits of Gibraltar, the rulers of Spain were waiting to attack the Vikings with a fleet of vessels, armed with Greek fire.[1] Bjorn had to fight his way past the Saracens (a term used at the time by Christians to describe Arabs), and during this epic battle, he lost 40 of his ships and much of his loot, but he managed to escape with his life and return to Sweden.

Not long after his return from the Mediterranean, Bjorn accompanied Ivar the Boneless to Northumbria to avenge the death of their father. Once they had gained their revenge and executed King Aella, Bjorn returned to Scandinavia. There he and his remaining brothers divided up their father's kingdom, and Bjorn became the king of Sweden. Raiding had made Bjorn Ironside a wealthy man, and after his return from England, he settled down in his new kingdom and lived out the rest of his days in relative peace. Bjorn fathered two sons, Refil and Erik Bjornsson. After Bjorn's death, his son Erik inherited his throne.

[1] *Greek fire was an incendiary weapon used by the Eastern Roman (Byzantine) Empire that was first developed c. 672. The Byzantines typically used it in naval battles to great effect, as it could continue burning while floating on water. It provided a technological advantage and was responsible for many key Byzantine military victories. (https://en.wikipedia.org/wiki/Greek_fire)*

Chapter Six: Harald Fairhair – First King of Norway

Harald Fairhair is credited with being the first true king of Norway, and according to the Icelandic sagas, he ruled circa 872 to 930. Before Harald consolidated Norway under his control, the Scandinavian Peninsula was little more than a collection of minor Viking kingdoms.

Harald was the son of Halfdan the Black, one of the minor rulers on the peninsula and the descendent of a long line of Viking warriors. When Harald was approximately ten years old, his father died when his sleigh crashed through the thawing ice of a frozen lake and he drowned. Halfdan's untimely death meant that Harald inherited the minor kingdom of Vestfold on the Norwegian peninsula. The jarls, wealthy men who owned property and ships, in the kingdom, however, did not want to be ruled by a mere boy and challenged Harald's authority. But they underestimated the young king, and with the aid of his father's chief military advisor, Duke Guthorm, Harald, according to legend, was able to subjugate the troublesome jarls and keep control of his kingdom at the age of ten.

But what of his interesting moniker, and how did he go from being a minor ruler to being the first king of Norway? As the story goes,

Harald then fell in love with Gyda, the daughter of King Eirik of Hordaland, but she refused to marry him until he was king of all of Norway. Harald apparently responded by declaring that he would not cut his hair until he had achieved his goal of uniting Norway under his leadership, and had won Gyda's hand in marriage. True to his word, Harald set about uniting Norway, refusing to cut or comb his hair or trim his beard. This earned him the nickname "Harald Tanglehair.'

Over the next decade, Harald set about consolidating his power and waged war on all the minor kingdoms around him to bring them under his control. Little is known of the battles he waged during this time, but his military campaign finally culminated in the epic Battle of Hafrsfjord, where Harald faced his two remaining enemies, King Eirik of Hordaland and King Sulke of Rogaland. By then, Norway was basically divided into two factions, those who supported Harald and those who didn't. The Battle of Hafrsfjord was a bloody naval battle fought in Hafrsfjord between Harald's fleet and an enemy armada commanded by Norwegian rulers who wanted to retain their small kingdoms. The battle lasted almost the entire day and left the fjord littered with the remains of destroyed ships and dead warriors.

In her article written in 2016, "Bronze Swords of Hafrsfjord Tell a Legendary Tale of a Powerful King and a Great Battle," Kerry Sullivan gives a good description of the battle.

> His campaign culminates in the epic Battle of Hafrsfjord. News came in from the southland that the people of Hordaland and Rogaland, Agder and Thelemark, were gathering, and bringing together ships and weapons, and a great body of men. The leaders of this were Eirik king of Hordaland; Sulke king of Rogaland, and his brother Earl Sote: Kjotve the Rich, king of Agder, and his son Thor Haklang; and from Thelemark two brothers, Hroald Hryg and Had the Hard. Now when Harald got certain news of this, he assembled his forces, set his ships on the water, made himself ready with his men, and set out southwards along the coast,

gathering many people from every district. King Eirik heard of this when he came south of Stad; and having assembled all the men he could expect, he proceeded southwards to meet the force that he knew was coming to his help from the east. The whole met together north of Jadar, and went into Hafersfjord, where King Harald was waiting with his forces. A great battle began, which was both hard and long; but at last King Harald gained the day. There King Eirik fell, and King Sulke, with his brother Earl Sote. Thor Haklang, who was a great berserker, had laid his ship against King Harald's, and there was above all measure a desperate attack, until Thor Haklang fell, and his whole ship was cleared of men. Then King Kjotve fled to a little isle outside [Iceland], on which there was a good place of strength. Thereafter all his men fled, some to their ships, some up to the land; and the latter ran southwards over the country of Jadar.[1]

At the end of the day, Harald Fairhair emerged victorious. After ten long years of fighting, he had finally achieved his goals: he had united Norway under his rule and married his princess. He also cut his hair, and his nickname changed from Harald Tanglehair to Harald Fairhair.

According to some legends, Harald was a just and fair king, and he ruled Norway for more than 50 years, dying circa 933 at the age of 83, a very old man by Viking standards. But other sources are not so kind about Harald's legacy and describe him as a ruthless and petty king, who violently consolidated Norway and forced many Norwegians to leave their homeland and settle in newly discovered Iceland. He instituted widespread administrative and land reform and ordered the payment of land taxes. This did not endear him to the predominately farming population, and he was labeled a tyrant. During Harald's reign, many Norwegians fled Norway to seek new opportunities in places like the Hebrides, Orkney, Shetlands, and Iceland.

Be that as it may, what is undisputable is that Harald not only united Norway but founded a dynasty that ruled on and off throughout the Viking Age. Two of his sons, Eric Bloodaxe and Haakon the Good, succeeded him on the throne, and today Harald is remembered as the father of Norway and one of its greatest kings.

[1] https://www.ancient-origins.net/ancient-places-europe/bronze-swords-hafrsfjord-tell-legendary-tale-powerful-king-and-great-battle-020925

Chapter Seven: Eric Bloodaxe – Terrifying Family Killer

It was not only the sight of Viking warriors that was enough to scare vulnerable and unprotected settlements, but at the height of the Viking Age, the reputations of these mighty men preceded them and struck terror into the hearts of their victims. One such legendary warrior, who had a fearsome reputation, was Eric Bloodaxe.

Like so many Viking warriors, there is very little contemporary information about Erik Haraldsson, nicknamed Eric Bloodaxe, but his is one of the most famous names in Viking history, especially in the British Isles. Most of what is known about Eric Bloodaxe was written long after his death and is pieced together from information contained in the *Anglo-Saxon Chronicle*, Irish chronicles, Norwegian stories, and the Icelandic sagas. The Norse sagas depict Eric Bloodaxe as a ruthless, bloodthirsty barbarian whose savagery was legendary, even by Viking standards. His name alone conjures up terrifying images.

Eric Bloodaxe was the son of Harald Fairhair, the first king of Norway. Like most Vikings, Eric grew up in a harsh and violent environment. By the age of twelve, he was taking part in Viking raids and using violence to take what he wanted. But that is not what earned him his horrific nickname. According to legend, Eric killed most of his brothers to clear his path to the throne, and that is why he was called Bloodaxe. While the sagas call him "Bloodaxe," one of the Latin texts calls him Fratris Interfector (brother-killer), so it seems likely that "blood" in this context refers to family, just as today we refer to "blood relations" as distinct from relations by marriage or adoption.[1]

When his father died, Eric succeeded him as king of western Norway, but he only ruled for a few years. Having secured his throne through violence and bloodshed, Eric probably could not have settled down to a life of peace and quiet, even if he wanted to. Few details exist about his brief rule in Norway, but most accounts describe him as a harsh and unpopular monarch, When his younger brother, Haakon the Good, made a claim for the kingdom, with the support of Athelstan of Wessex, Eric Bloodaxe gave up his throne, without a fight, and moved to the British Isles. Having murdered his other brothers to claim the throne, it is unknown why he gave it up to Haakon. Perhaps he realized he didn't have enough support in Norway to win a battle against the combined forces of Haakon and Athelstan.

Unlike his ruthless older brother, Haakon did not kill his sibling, and Eric was able to flee Norway. He then turned his attention on the British Isles and established himself as ruler of the Viking kingdom of Northumbria.

From his base in York, Eric frequently raided settlements in Scotland and around the Irish Sea. His raids were mainly driven by a need to increase his wealth, as Northumbria was not rich enough to support Eric and his followers, but he was probably also driven by a desire for violence and plunder. Eric ruled Northumbria circa 947 to 948 and then again from 952 to 954, but he was clearly not strong enough to hold his position with any surety. He constantly had to contend with attacks from his rivals in Dublin and the kingdom of

Wessex, both of whom were also intent on expanding their own territories to increase their wealth and power.

As the old adage goes, "You live by the sword, you die by the sword," and it was almost inevitable that Eric Bloodaxe would die in battle. He met his untimely end at Stainmore, north of York in a remote area of the Pennines, in 954, reputedly killed by a man named Maccus, possibly the son of King Olaf of Dublin. Eric's death ended independent Viking rule in Northumbria.

[1] Eric Bloodaxe By Gareth Williams
http://www.bbc.co.uk/history/ancient/vikings/bloodaxe_01.shtml

Chapter Eight: Egil Skallagrimsson – Warrior Poet

Egil Skallagrimsson was a Viking warrior and one of the greatest Scandinavian poets, or skalds. His family immigrated to Iceland to escape the tyrannical rule of King Harald Fairhair, and he was born there circa 910. According to legend (based mostly on his own poetry), he composed his first poem at the very young age of three. His life and adventures are recorded in *Egil's Saga* as part of the *Saga of the Icelanders*, an account of Icelandic history most likely written by another great Icelandic poet, Snorri Sturluson.[1]

Storytelling, skaldic poetry, and the reciting of sagas, especially those about the exploits of Viking heroes, was deeply ingrained in Norse society. During Viking feasts, Scandinavian bards, called skalds, recited epic poems or sagas that praised the brave deeds of Viking warriors and their prowess in battle. These sagas were important to the Vikings, because before they converted to Christianity, they had no written records of significant events. Their history was passed on orally through the generations, and the great sagas were memorized and recited by the skalds. These sagas were often incredibly long and detailed, and many, like the *Saga of Erik the Red* and the *Saga of the Greenlanders*, were only written down long after the events that they describe, by which time they had been altered and embellished. Unfortunately, many of the great sagas and skaldic poems have been lost to history. But those that have survived are valuable historical resources for scholars. Not only do they give great insight into the lives of the Vikings and their mighty deeds, but they also provide a glimpse into how the Vikings viewed themselves and how they wanted to be remembered. Egil Skallagrimsson is a prime example of this.

The poetry that Egil Skallagrimsson and his peers specialized in, skaldic poetry as it is now termed, was most importantly praise poetry, designed to commemorate kings and other prominent people, often in the form of long poems. But the poems also often treat exploits of the poet himself, this time in extempore single verses commenting on specific situations and always in a highly self-congratulatory tone. They are extremely complex metrically and use a highly ornate metaphoric language—their complexity presumably helped ensure that it would be remembered even in an age that was for all intents and purposes without writing. But because it is so concerned with praise, it can tell us a great deal about the qualities the Vikings themselves held dear. [2]

It is important to note that Egil was not a meek and soft-spoken man, as one might imagine a poet to be, but rather a typical Viking warrior who recognized the importance and value of poetry, and had a talent for composing great poems. In fact, he had such a talent for it that it got him out of trouble a few times and literally saved his head. Egil also had a sizeable ego and often praised his own exploits in his poetry. Much of what we know about Egil was written by Egil himself but he also features prominently in the Icelandic sagas.

According to the Icelandic sagas, Egil Skallagrimsson composed his first poem when he was three to impress the guests at a feast. His father had forbidden him to attend the feast but he went anyway, and after he recited his poem, the guests were so impressed that his father couldn't be angry with him. But Egil could also be violent and the bloodthirsty side of his character was not quite so endearing to everyone. He first killed someone when he was six or seven. This incident apparently took place when he was playing a ball game against a boy called Grim. After a disagreement, where Egil swung a bat at Grim and Grim pushed him to the ground making the other children laugh, Egil fetched an ax and split Grim's skull in two. This led to a larger fight in which seven people were killed. Egil's father was angry with him, but his mother praised his actions and declared that he had the traits of a true Viking and would make a good warrior. This incident illustrates how important respect and the Viking warrior ideals were to Norse society.

After the death of King Harald Fairhair, Egil's family returned to Norway, but it was not long before Egil came into conflict with Harald's son, Eric Bloodaxe. Once again, Egil left Norway and he, along with his brother, Thorolf, spent a number of years raiding and fighting as mercenaries in the British Isles. When Thorolf was killed in Scotland, Egil decided to return to Norway to marry his sister-in-law and claim his brother's inheritance. But his return once again led to conflict with Eric Bloodaxe, and during a dispute, Eric's son, Rognvald, was killed. Egil was banished from Norway and took refuge in Iceland. But this was not the end of his trouble with Eric Bloodaxe.

While on a voyage, Egil's ship was wrecked on the English coast near York and was captured by Eric Bloodaxe. Legend has it that in order to save his head, Egil composed an epic skaldic poem praising Eric and his rule. The king was so impressed that he not only spared Egil's life but also ended his banishment. The poem became known as the "Head-Ransom" poem. Egil's greatest poem, however, had far more tragic roots. After his son Bodvarr drowned, he composed a poem called "Sonatorrek," which is considered to be one of the finest examples of Viking poetry. Egil was both a great poet and Viking warrior, but unlike so many of his contemporaries, he did not meet a warrior's death, instead succumbing to old age and dying at the age of 80.

[1] *Snorri Sturluson is one of the best-known Icelandic skalds. He was born in Iceland in 1179 and became a wealthy and renowned poet and law-speaker, the man in a settlement whose duty was to know the laws of the settlement and those of broader Viking society. Snorri wrote the* Prose Edda, *which together with the* Poetic Edda *(written by Saemunder Sigfusson) has given modern historians much insight into Norse mythology. As a poet, Snorri would have heard many legends and tales that at the time only existed in oral form and may have decided to preserve these tales in the* Prose Edda. *He also composed the* Heimskringla, *a history of the kings of Norway from the 9th century to 1177. Snorri Sturluson is a good example of the importance of the skald in Scandinavian society. Without skalds, much of the history and culture of the Vikings would have been lost.*

[2] Christina van Nolcken, Egil Skallagrimsson and the Viking Ideal

Chapter Nine: Sweyn Forkbeard – The Forgotten King of England

Sweyn Forkbeard, so named for his long cleft beard, was born circa 960 and was the son of the Danish King Harald Bluetooth. His life is depicted in several important medieval chronicles outside of Scandinavia, like the 12th-century *Deeds of the Bishops of Hamburg*, written by German scholar Adam of Bremen, or the magnum opus of John of Wallingford, simply titled *Chronica*. The 13th-century English monk, healer, and author tried to capture the history of Sweyn's conquest of Britain, portraying him as a merciless and godless figure, typical of the image of Northern invaders in early medieval England.[1]

Circa 986, Sweyn Forkbeard became king of Denmark by seizing the throne from his father and forcing him into exile. But his rule was short-lived. When he led his army in a campaign to capture London, King Eric of Sweden took advantage of Forkbeard's absence and claimed the throne of Denmark. This was a disaster for Forkbeard, because not only did he lose the Danish throne, his campaign in England was also unsuccessful and he was forced into exile in Scotland.

Forkbeard recovered the Danish throne when Eric died circa 994. For a while he was content to merely rule Denmark, but after a few years, Forkbeard once again launched an attack on English shores. Many historians believe that Forkbeard's attack on England was in retaliation for the St. Brice's Day Massacre. This brutal attack took place in 1002 when the English King Ethelred II ordered the massacre of Danes living in England. Historians believe that Ethelred may have ordered the massacre because he feared the Danes could rise up against him. Another theory is that he was tired of being attacked by the Vikings and took his frustration out on the Danish population in England. Apparently, no one was spared, and men, women, and children were all killed. When news of the massacre reached Forkbeard, he swore that he would avenge his countrymen and attacked England in 1003.

This time Forkbeard met little resistance as he spent two years rampaging through the English countryside. He then returned to Denmark in 1005 to deal with a severe famine. This was, however, not the last the English saw of Forkbeard. In the summer of 1013, accompanied by his son Cnut, he again attacked England with a substantial army. It did not take long for Northumbria and the whole Danelaw to submit to him. This was not due to the strength of his army or his military prowess, but rather because the power of the English throne, under the weak and ineffectual King Ethelred, was collapsing, and the local English lords were not prepared to be slaughtered in his defense. Instead they supported Sweyn Forkbeard in his campaign to capture the throne of England. As Sweyn's power grew, the legitimate king of England became weaker, and when London fell to the Vikings, Ethelred fled to the Isle of Wight and then later to Normandy.

Sweyn Forkbeard was eventually crowned king of England on Christmas Day 1014, but here too his rule was short-lived. He died a mere five weeks later, and King Ethelred returned to reclaim his throne. The exact circumstances of his death are unknown, but sources suggest he fell from his horse.

Sweyn Forkbeard's rule may not have lasted long, but that was not the end of his legacy in England. Sweyn's son, Cnut, had fled England when Ethelred reasserted his right to the throne, but he soon returned and became king of England in 1016, after the death of Ethelred and his son Edmund Ironside. Cnut and his sons, Harold Harefoot and Harthacnut, ruled England for the next 26 years.

[1] https://www.thevintagenews.com/2018/03/22/sweyn-forkbeard/

Chapter Ten: King Olaf Tryggvason and the Rise of Christianity in Norway

Little is known about the early life of Olaf Tryggvason. He was born circa 960 and was the son of Tryggvi Olafsson, king of Viken, and became a mighty Viking warrior, who acquired great wealth and fame by raiding and plundering throughout Europe. Being a Norseman, he would have been raised to worship the Viking pagan gods. At the time, however, Christianity was already the dominant religion in Europe and it is believed that King Olaf converted to Christianity during his campaign in Britain around 994. When he returned to his homeland, he brought his new faith with him and became the first Christian king of Norway.

 The Vikings may have loved their pagan gods but it was not unusual during this time for Vikings to become Christians, and by the end of the Viking Age, most had converted and were baptized and buried in the faith. One of the factors that made the Vikings adopt Christianity was not religious beliefs but rather practical reasons. Viking traders were beginning to suffer losses because Christian traders and countries began to discriminate against Muslims and pagans. To solve this problem and continue trading in Europe, many Vikings traders merely adopted the signs of Christianity outwardly to protect their business interests. They would wear a cross when trading with Christians but replaced it with Thor's hammer when they returned to their homes. Olaf Tryggvason was, however, a true believer in all things Christian.

In 996, when Olaf returned to Norway from raiding in England, he heard that the current ruler, Jarl Haakon, was becoming increasingly unpopular with the people, and once he arrived, he joined a rebellion against the ruler. After Haakon had been killed, Olaf was proclaimed king by the Althing. As the first Christian king of Norway, he then brutally set about converting the predominantly pagan population to Christianity. Pagan temples were destroyed and churches were built in their place. Those who refused to convert were killed, tortured, maimed, or banished. After bringing Christianity to Norway, King Olaf was determined to spread his new religion's beliefs to the outlying colonies of Iceland and Greenland. But while he may have succeeded in forcefully converting Norway to Christianity, Greenland and Iceland were beyond the reach of his sword, and he had to use other means to convince the settlers to convert.

King Olaf sent missionaries to Iceland in the late 990s, but they met with limited success. He then tried a more aggressive approach and cut off trade between Iceland and Norway, and also threatened to kill Icelanders living in Norway. King Olaf's actions led to growing tensions between pagans and Christians in Iceland. To prevent a civil war, the adoption of Christianity was put to a vote and adopted at the Althing in the year 1000.

Unfortunately for King Olaf, by the time the Icelanders adopted Christianity, the Greenlanders had already left the island. Conversion in Greenland was a more gradual and voluntary process, and it was never mandated by the Althing. One of the reasons for this may have been that Erik the Red, who established the Viking settlement on Greenland, never embraced Christianity and remained a committed pagan until he died.

This might have been a problem for King Olaf, but an opportunity presented itself when Leif Erikson, explorer and son of Erik the Red, visited Norway around 997. Before Leif made his voyage to Norway, he, like the rest of his family and most of the other settlers, worshiped pagan gods.

It was not unusual at the time for young Norsemen to serve as retainers in the royal household, and the Greenlanders were still very much tied to their Norwegian homeland. This visit was an opportunity for Leif to make political connections and form alliances that would place him in good standing in the future. It was also an opportunity for King Olaf to find a convert to spread Christianity to Greenland. When Leif arrived in Norway, he was welcomed into the court of King Olaf, and it appears that the king took quite a shine to the young Greenlander. The time Leif spent with King Olaf was to have a lasting influence, not only on Leif, but also on the settlement of Greenland as it was during his visit to Norway that Leif converted to Christianity.

In Leif, King Olaf had found a young man who was held in high esteem in Greenland and who was able to influence and convert the Greenlanders to the Christian faith. Before Leif and his crew returned to Greenland, they all converted and were baptized. King Olaf then gave Leif the task of spreading the faith to Greenland. According to the *Saga of Erik the Red*, he even sent a priest back to Greenland with Leif.

Using his influence and reputation as a man of fair judgment and honesty, Leif was able to convert many Greenlanders, including his mother, Thjodhild, who had been a life-long pagan. In fact, she became so passionate about her new religion that she commissioned the first church built in Greenland. In 1932, a group of Danish archaeologists excavating Brattahlid (Erik the Red's homestead) found the remains of what they assume is Thjodhild's church. The church could hold between 20 and 30 worshipers, was surrounded by a wall to keep out farm animals, and was located close to a communal hall, where people could meet and play board games.

Later, in 1961, a small horseshoe-shaped chapel was also found on the site as well as the skeletal remains of 144 people.

King Olaf, unfortunately, did not live long enough to see Leif fulfill his mission. He was killed in 1000 at the Battle of Svolder when his small fleet was attacked by the combined superior power of the Swedish, Danish, and Wendish fleets, together with the ships of Jarl Haakon's sons. Apparently, Olaf fought to the bitter end before jumping into the water, never being seen again.

Chapter Eleven: Harald Hardrada – The Last Great Viking Ruler

Harald Sigurdsson, better known as Harald Hardrada (meaning "hard ruler"), was king of Norway from 1046 until his death on the battlefield of Stamford Bridge in 1066. Harald is often referred to as the "Last Great Viking Ruler." He was a renowned military leader with ambitions to expand his kingdom, and it was this quest for power that ultimately led to his downfall when he attempted to claim the throne of England in 1066.

The youngest of three brothers, Harald was born in Ringerike, Norway in 1015. His father was Sigurd Syr, one of the wealthiest chieftains in the country. Some historians claim that Harald was also a descendent of King Harald Fairhair, but there is no proof to back this up.

In 1030, Harald supported his brother, Olaf, in his bid to claim the Norwegian throne from the Danish King Cnut. Unfortunately, the Norwegians were defeated at the Battle of Stiklestad and Olaf was killed. Harald fled Norway, first going north to Sweden and then east to Kiev and beyond. During the 1030s, Harald raided and fought throughout Europe, traveling as far as Constantinople and Jerusalem. He became a well-known military leader who fought in the service of the Byzantines and became a very wealthy man. In 1042, he returned to Kiev and married Elisabeth, daughter of Yaroslav the Wise, the prince of Kiev.

In 1045, Harald returned to Scandinavia to attempt to reclaim the Norwegian throne. By then, Cnut was no longer interested in Norway and had focused his attention on England. In his absence, Cnut had left Magnus the Good, Olaf's illegitimate son, to rule Norway. Harald and Magnus, who was his nephew, did not want to go to war with each other, so instead they agreed to share the power. Or rather, Harald bought himself a share of the throne by paying half his sizeable wealth to a bankrupt Magnus. This arrangement did not last long as Magnus died in 1047. He had no heir, and Cnut never returned to claim the throne, so Harald finally became king of Norway. But Harald was clearly an ambitious man, and he wanted to spread his power and influence beyond the borders of his homeland and so declared himself king of Denmark as well. This led to twenty years of conflict and warfare between Norway and Denmark. In 1064, a peace agreement was reached between the two kingdoms.

When he was no longer at war with Denmark, and like so many Vikings before him, Harald Hardrada turned his attention to the British Isles. When Edward the Confessor (King of England 1045 to 1066) died without an heir, Harald believed he had a claim to the English throne, but it passed to Harald Godwinson, the son of one of Edward's advisers. Harald Hardrada, however, was prepared to fight for the right to rule England. He formed an alliance with one of Edward's brothers, Tostig, and together they invaded England in September 1066. Hardrada and Godwinson faced each other on the battlefield at Stamford Bridge. Hardrada's army was vastly outnumbered, and it was Godwinson who emerged victorious when Hardrada was killed by an arrow to the neck. Godwinson's victory was, however, short-lived, and approximately a month later, he was defeated by William the Conqueror at the Battle of Hastings, with the course of English history changing forever.

Timeline of Heroes and Villains

790s – Beginning of the Viking Age

Early 9th Century – Viking warlord, Ragnar Lothbrok, is born

Circa 845 – Ragnar Lothbrok sacks Paris

Circa 860 – Bjorn Ironside raids and plunders the Mediterranean

Circa 865 – Great Heathen Army, led by Ivar the Boneless, invades England and kills King Aella of Northumbria to avenge the death of his father, Ragnar Lothbrok

Circa 870 – Ivar the Boneless most likely dies in Dublin

Circa 872 to 930 – Harald Fairhair consolidates his power and rules Norway

910 – Warrior poet Egil Skallagrimsson is born

Circa 947 to 948 – Eric Bloodaxe rules Northumbria for first time

Circa 952 to 954 – Eric Bloodaxe rules Northumbria for second time until his death at Stainmore

Circa 960 – Sweyn Forkbeard is born in Denmark, and Olaf Tryggvason is born in Norway

Circa 986 – Sweyn Forkbeard seizes the throne of Denmark from his father but soon loses it to King Eric of Sweden

Circa 990 - Egil Skallagrimsson dies

994 – Sweyn Forkbeard regains the throne of Denmark on the death of King Eric of Sweden

996 – Olaf Tryggvason becomes the first Christian king of Norway

1000 – King Olaf dies at the Battle of Svolder

Circa 1002 – St Brice's Day Massacre

Circa 1003 – Sweyn Forkbeard attacks England

Circa 1005 – Sweyn Forkbeard returns to Denmark

Circa 1013 – Sweyn Forkbeard attacks England again December 1014 – Sweyn Forkbeard becomes king of England; his reign lasts 5 weeks

1015 – Sweyn Forkbeard dies

1015 – Harald Sigurdsson, better known as Harald Hardrada, was born in Ringerike, Norway

1016 – Forkbeard's son, Cnut, becomes king of England. He and his sons, Harold Harefoot and Harthacunt, rule England for the next 26 years

1045– Harald Hardrada becomes king of Norway in conjunction with his nephew Magnus the Good

1047 – Magnus the Good dies without an heir, and Harald Hardrada becomes the sole king of Norway. Claims the throne of Denmark as well, and this leads to twenty years of war and conflict between the two kingdoms.

1064 – Harald Hardrada makes peace with Denmark

September 1066 – Harald Hardrada invades England and attempts to seize the throne from Harald Godwinson. Hardrada is killed on the battlefield at Stamford Bridge.

1066 – End of the Viking Age

Section Three: The Viking Age of Exploration

The Vikings were, without a doubt, ruthless warriors, and their propensity for violence is well documented. It can be argued that they lived in violent and brutal times, but even by the standards of the day, their level of brutality was often considered extreme and they were feared by many. The sight of their dragon boats gliding silently upriver was enough to spread terror throughout a region.

The history and legacy of the Vikings is very much tied to the battles they fought, the territories they conquered, and the mighty warriors they produced, but there is more to their story than centuries of fighting, raiding, and plundering. The Vikings were also great explorers who discovered and settled new lands. They ventured far from their homelands in search of wealth and power, and many of them never returned to the lands of their birth, instead finding new areas to settle and colonize. The Hebrides, British Isles, Faroe Islands, and parts of Russia and Europe were all occupied by the mighty Norsemen at times during the Viking Age. But it was not just the allure of power and wealth that drove the Vikings to seek out new lands; it was also a sense of adventure. They were not just occupiers and colonizers of existing kingdoms; they also settled untamed territories and were the first Europeans to set foot on the North American continent.

Their indomitable spirit and tenacity are clearly demonstrated through their ability to build lives for themselves in lands that most people would consider too uninviting and marginal for settlement. But the Vikings did not let things like climate and rough seas stand in the way of exploration and expansion, and their legacy is not just one of violence and mayhem but also innovation and adaptability. The impact that their exploration and settlement of Iceland, Greenland, and Vinland (a brief Viking settlement along the coast of North America, the exact location of which is still unknown but could have been as far north as Newfoundland or as far south as Cape Cod) had on world history should not be overshadowed by their propensity for violence and plunder.

The marauding tendencies of Vikings certainly had a significant bearing on world history and on the communities they attacked. But no conqueror remains unaffected by the people they conquer or the lands they colonize. Part of the Vikings' success was the fact that they could adapt. The culture of the Viking Age was strong, independent, vibrant, and rich in tradition. It was good at copying, adapting, developing, and creating, at times intertwining with foreign ideas. The many points of contact with other nations meant that well-informed and well-traveled Scandinavians were familiar with a variety of nationalities, environments, and cultures. Their tolerance of other cultures was presumably an important factor in the Scandinavians astonishing ability to establish themselves as traders, conquerors, or colonists in new countries.[1]

The Vikings took the most useful aspects of other cultures and assimilated them into their own society. This ensured that their legacy is so much more than that of a warrior nation. Their culture of innovation and adaptability allowed them to live and thrive throughout the known world at the time and leave a lasting mark on history.

[1] Else Rosendahl and Preben Meulengracht Sorensen, *The Viking Culture*, The Cambridge History of Scandinavia, Issue 1 (Knut Helle, ed., 2003), p. 121

Chapter Twelve: Master Shipbuilders and Navigators

New territories offered the Norsemen more resources and greater political freedom; there they enjoyed fewer laws, taxes, and social constraints. Establishing new settlements also offered the more adventurous Vikings access to a better life. Uninhabited territories, such as Iceland and Greenland, had an abundance of natural resources, farmland, and grazing for livestock. As in most cases of mass migration, it was a combination of factors that drove the Vikings across the ocean, but without advancing technology, and the influence that this had on shipbuilding and navigation, their voyages of conquest and exploration would not have been possible.

Technology played a pivotal role in the Viking Age of expansion. Although no written historical records about the settlement of Iceland, Greenland, and Vinland exist from the time, the sagas that were written some two hundred years later give us insight into how the Vikings were able to traverse the treacherous ocean to reach these remote areas.

The Scandinavians were the most advanced shipbuilders and navigators in Europe at the time, and they were able to cross many nautical miles of open seas in their longboats. The design of the Viking longboats enabled them to reach a height of naval power unheard of before in the region. The typical Norse vessel was wide and stable with a shallow draught that enabled it to travel upriver and land on beaches, but it was also a good seagoing vessel. The boats were light and fast, and there was nothing to rival them at the time.

Longboats were clinker built. This meant that the planks of the hull were not laid edge to edge but rather overlapped each other. The seams between the planks were caulked over with tar-soaked animal hair. This design made the longboats both strong and flexible. The shipbuilders predominately used oak as it was very durable, but other types of timber were also used. These vessels, rigged with large square sails made of rough cloth and fitted with between 6 and 30 rowing benches, were able to cross the treacherous waters of the open ocean where ice floes, icebergs, and frozen rigging were a constant danger. The longboats were an integral part of Viking life, and the Norsemen took pride in their vessels; they gave them names, decorated them with carvings, and adorned them with dragon heads. Viking enemies often referred to the longboats as "dragon ships" because of their dragon-shaped bow.

The Vikings used their vessels to great effect to raid, plunder, and spread their influence throughout the known world. The long, narrow, light boats with their shallow hulls could not only cross oceans but could also sail upriver to attack inland settlements. During the 9th century, the longboats played a pivotal role in the age of Viking expansion. With these remarkable boats, the Vikings were able to travel upriver and attack inland towns and cities such as Rouen in 841 and Hamburg in 845. The longboats were fast and easy to maneuver and could glide easily through deep or shallow waters, making quick getaways after surprise attacks on vulnerable settlements. The longboats, with their dragon heads and drawings of wild animals on the sails, were also frightening to behold. But the longboats were not just good for hit-and-run raids; they were also used to transport troops to battles and could be tied together to form floating fighting platforms for offshore battles. These boats were also used in various other ways, like trade, the exploration of new territories, fishing, seal and whale hunting, or to transport livestock, goods, and people over vast stretches of open water.

There were a number of different types of longboat designs, and mostly they were classified by the number of rowing positions on board. The Karvi was the smallest Viking longboat and had between 6 and 16 benches. This was a general-purpose vessel that was used for fishing and trade, but could also be used in battle. The Snekkja had at least 20 rowing benches and could carry a crew of approximately 41 men. Snekkjas were useful in raids because they were light and could be beached or easily carried across portages. Skeids were larger warships and had more than 30 rowing benches, carrying around 70 to 80 men. The Norsemen also built boats specifically designed to carry cargo, these were known as Knarr. The Knarr had a hull that was wider, deeper and shorter than a fighting longboat. It could carry more cargo and needed a smaller crew to operate it.

In 1926, Norwegian shipbuilders in Korgen built a replica of the type of longboat that Leif Erikson would have used on his journey to Vinland. The ship, named the Leif Erikson, was 42 feet long modified Knarr, and Captain Gerhard Folgero and his crew sailed it from Bergen, Norway to North America. The ship stopped at the Shetland Islands, Faroe Islands, Iceland, and Greenland before crossing the Atlantic. On July 20, 1926, they docked at St Johns, Newfoundland. From there they sailed south along the coast to Boston, Massachusetts and finally reached Duluth in Minnesota on June 23, 1927. It was not an easy voyage, and the ship encountered heavy seas and even became ice-locked near Greenland, but this voyage proved that the Vikings were more than capable of sailing from Greenland to North America with their longboats.

Another useful tool in the Viking seafarer's arsenal were their exceptional navigational techniques that allowed them to explore the ocean. They could travel far from land, establish trading posts in new territories, and create settlements in areas that had until then been inaccessible. While Viking navigational techniques are not well understood, it is clear that they were experts at judging speed, currents, and wind direction, as well as predicting the tides.

The Vikings may not have had any of the navigational tools that are available to modern sailors, such as computers and GPS technology, but they had a rich maritime tradition and an outstanding knowledge of the sea. They didn't even have access to a basic compass, but their knowledge of coastlines, currents, navigational markers, whales, and seabirds all played a role in their navigational techniques and enabled them to form mental maps of their journeys. These skills were passed on from one generation to the next, and each generation would have improved their navigational techniques and built on the knowledge acquired from their fathers and grandfathers.

Norsemen used their five senses, practical experience, and to some degree intuition to aid in navigation on the open waters. Along coastlines and in sight of land, they would use navigational markers, such as hills or unusually shaped rock formations, to ascertain their position and the direction in which they wished to sail. They also used nature and the abundance of sea life to aid navigation. For instance, the sailors would observe whales swimming or feeding in certain areas or currents. They knew that at certain times of the year whales would be found in particular parts of the ocean, and so they could use whale pods to orientate themselves. But keeping a close eye on nature was not enough—the Vikings also had to be able to find their way to shore even through dense fog and mist. Here a good ear was needed, and many Norsemen could identify different bird calls and the sounds of waves breaking on the shore long before they saw the actual coastline. In this way they could guide their longboats safely home and avoid dangerous, rocky shorelines.

They may also have used simple tools such as a plumb bob (a weight on the end of a line) to measure ocean depth and a basic latitude finder that floated in a bucket of water. This comprised of a circle of wood with a perpendicular stick of wood (or gnomon) stuck into it. The sun cast the gnomon's shadow on the circle of wood and helped the Vikings determine latitude. But the Vikings also had to be able to find their way in cloudy weather, and one possible navigational tool that they could have used to do this was a crystal known as a "Sunstone." These sunstones are mentioned in the *Saga of King Olaf* and were apparently key to navigating in poor weather. Sunstones split a beam of light, separating polarized light from the main beam.[1] By looking at the sky through these crystals, it is possible to see the rings of polarized light that surround the sun even in stormy weather. Being able to identify the sun's location would have given the Vikings a point of reference during long ocean crossings.

But sailing over vast distances in open longboats took more than just remarkable shipbuilding ability, navigational skills, and seamanship, all of which the Norsemen clearly had in abundance—it also took courage. Traversing the deep sea was not for the fainthearted and the men and women who made these voyages were remarkable people. They had the courage to sail across treacherous open waters and brave storms, fog, and ice to settle new lands. Women and children traveled alongside their husbands and fathers to colonize new lands and endured great hardships, pain, and deprivation without complaint. They must have also been very resourceful to carve out a new life for their families in harsh and unforgiving environments.

[1] http://www.sciencemag.org/news/2018/04/viking-seafarers-may-have-navigated-legendary-crystals

Chapter Thirteen: Erik the Red – Mighty Warrior and Brave Explorer

The Vikings' ability to adapt to their environment and establish settlements in areas that by most standards would be considered harsh and inhospitable, and the impact this had on world history, is clearly illustrated by the adventures of Erik the Red and his son, Leif Erikson.

Erik Thorvaldsson, better known by his nickname Erik the Red because of his flaming red hair and beard, perfectly fits the popular image of the fearsome Viking warrior who spent his days raiding and plundering, and his nights feasting, drinking, and regaling his fellow Norsemen with tall tales of his daring exploits.

Erik has been described in the sagas as a large, strong man, who could wield a double-edged sword or ax with skill and accuracy. He was by all accounts a mighty warrior and also a violent man with a short temper, who did not shy away from confrontation. He was clearly not averse to killing, in battle or in the heat of an argument. In his youth, he did his fair share of looting, joining his fellow Norsemen as they ruthlessly preyed on weaker communities, small settlements, churches, and monasteries. But he was also an adventurer who changed the face of the Viking world. Erik the Red's greatest achievement was not on the battlefield. His legacy is the discovery and settlement of Greenland.

Erik the Red was born circa 950 in Norway as the son of a Norwegian farmer, Thorvald Asvaldsson. When Thorvald was found guilty of murder and banished from Norway, the family moved to Iceland. Erik grew up on a typical Icelandic farm. By the time he was twelve, he was considered a man and was expected to do his fair share of the hard, physical labor that was required to feed the family. He learned how to hunt and fish, as well as raise livestock and plants and harvest crops, and Erik grew up to be a successful farmer.

After the death of his father, Erik married Thjodhild Jorundsdottir, and together they moved to another part of Iceland, named Haukadal. Thjodhild came from a wealthy family, and it is believed that the property where they settled after their marriage may have been part of the marriage dowry or an inheritance from her family. Most Vikings married young; brides could be as young as twelve, and by the age of twenty, most Viking men and women were already married. Marriages were usually arranged by the parents, and a marriage was seen not only as a union between husband and wife but as a contract between two families. When the parents agreed on a marriage, the groom's family paid a bride price, and when the marriage took place, the bride's father paid a dowry. This meant that both families had a financial interest in the marriage.

Erik made good use of his marriage dowry, and at Haukadal, he prospered. He built a farm called Eiriksstadir and started a family. He had four children who survived to adulthood: three sons, Thorvald, Leif, and Thorstein, and a daughter, Freydis. For a while, the family was doing well and life was good, but unfortunately, things were not destined to stay that way for long.

Erik was known to have a fiery temper and this soon led to conflict with his neighbors that quickly escalated to violence. By the 980s, Erik owned a number of thralls (slaves) who worked on his farm. One day several of his thralls, who were working the land, accidentally triggered a landslide that crushed his neighbor Valthjof's house. One of Valthjof's clansmen, Eyiolf the Foul, killed Erik's thralls. In retaliation, Erik killed Eyiolf the Foul and another man named Holmgang-Hrafn. Erik was then outlawed from Haukadal and the surrounding area, but not from the entirety of Iceland. He was forced to leave his prosperous farm and move his family farther north to the Icelandic island of Oxney.

But this altercation with Eyiolf the Foul and his kinsmen was only the beginning of Erik's troubles in Iceland. Sometime around 982, Erik entrusted his setstokkr (large beams with Viking symbols carved on them that held mystical value for the Vikings as part of their pagan religion) to his friend and fellow settler, Thorgest, for safekeeping. These setstokkr were very precious to Erik as they were a family heirloom. He had inherited the setstokkr from his father, who had bought them all the way from Norway when he was banished to Iceland.

As the story goes, when Erik's new home in Oxney was complete, he returned to claim his setstokkr, but Thorgest refused to give them back. Erik then took the setstokkr by force and set off back to his own farm. But Erik was a savvy man and an experienced warrior, and he feared retaliation from Thorgest. So instead of returning directly to his farm, Erik set up an ambush, and during the ensuing fight, two of Thorgest's sons were killed by Erik. This act could not go unpunished, and once again Erik's fate was decided by the village men. He was found guilty of murder, and this time he was outlawed from the entirety of Iceland. Fortunately for Erik, he was not banished for life; he was only exiled for three years and his family was able to keep their farm.

For many Vikings this would have been a devastating blow, but Erik was a resourceful man and he turned adversity into opportunity. He spent his years in exile exploring Greenland, and what he found was a land with a similar climate to Iceland and enough resources to support a permanent settlement. [1]

In 982, within a few months of being banished, Erik and his crew of Vikings set sail from Sneefellsjokull, planning to locate and explore the landmass that lay to the west of Iceland. One of the reasons that Erik the Red may have chosen to explore Greenland could be related to the hillingar effect. This is a weather phenomenon that at times makes a mirage of Greenland visible from the mountains of northwestern Iceland, even though it is below the geometric horizon.[2] Since Erik grew up in Hornstrandir, which is in the remote northwestern part of the island, it is quite possible that he had on occasion seen the landmass that lay to the west of Iceland and was curious about it. He may also have hoped it would be a better alternative for him than Iceland, having twice fallen foul of the law there.

Erik and his crew sailed approximately 180 miles across the icy waters of the Atlantic in their open longboats to reach the shores of Greenland. Their first sight of the landmass would most likely have been the towering outline of the east coast. However, due to the large ice banks along the shoreline, they would not have been able to make landfall there. For many people, this would have been a daunting sight, maybe even enough to make them turn back, but Erik and his crew were not deterred by Greenland's icy landscape. When they couldn't make landfall on the eastern side of the island, they rounded Cape Farewell and sailed until they found a place to go ashore on the west coast. Their first priority once they made landfall would have been establishing a place to spend the winter.

According to the *Saga of Erik the Red*, the Norsemen spent the first winter at a place they named Eiriksey (Erik's Island). When the spring came and the ground thawed slightly, they set about exploring the vast landmass. It is estimated that the Vikings covered over 6,000 miles during the foursailing seasons (spring/summer) that they spent exploring Greenland during Erik the Red's exile. They traveled up the fjords and moved farther inland to a place that Erik named Eriksfjord. Here they found arable land and lush grazing. The second winter they spent in another area, this time in a place named

Eiriksholmar. (These names reveal a lot about Erik's character and how he viewed himself.) During their three years in Greenland, the Vikings explored as far north as Snaefell and Hrafnsfjord.

To people nowadays, Greenland may seem like an odd choice as a place to settle. These days there is very little arable land to farm and not much grazing for livestock, not to mention the climate is harsh and inhospitable. But to the Vikings, the new land they explored had a similar climate to what they were accustomed to in Iceland. Like Iceland, the fjords in Greenland froze in the winter and snow covered most of ground, but when spring came and the snow melted, it exposed the lush grazing and arable land that lay beneath the icy layer. Another factor that added to Greenland's appeal for the Norsemen was that it was uninhabited. There were no indigenous people or other settlers living around the fjords or along the coast of the southern part of the island. When the Norse established their settlements, they found the remains of earlier Inuit settlements in the area, but they had long since moved on.

After three years exploring Greenland, Erik briefly returned to Iceland to gather a group of settlers to establish the first European settlement on the icy landmass. After his return, Erik spent the winter recruiting followers and preparing to return to Greenland, not as an explorer with a crew of hardened men, but as a colonizer with a party of three hundred men, women, and children. The settlers who accompanied Erik to Greenland would have had various reasons for leaving Iceland. By then Iceland was heavily populated and some would have been seeking greener pastures and an opportunity to increase their wealth. Others may have been escaping the law. But whatever their reasons, these people were willing to give up their entire lives in Iceland to venture into the unknown and start again. They took with them their household belongings, tools, seeds to grow crops, livestock, and everything they would need to start a new life in a harsh and unsettled territory.

In the summer of 985, Erik the Red and his followers sailed for Greenland and a new life. But making the journey from Iceland to

Greenland wouldn't have been easy. Crossing the vast open ocean in Viking longboats was a treacherous and risky venture. The settlers had to deal with rough seas, inclement weather, and large icebergs. Ultimately only fourteen vessels made it safely to Greenland. The others were blown off course and wrecked or returned to Iceland.

Making it to Greenland was an achievement in its own right, but it was merely the beginning of the adventure for the settlers, and once they landed life did not get any easier. In the early years of the settlement, every day was still a struggle for survival. Homesteads had to be built, crops needed to be planted, and the men had to hunt and fish to feed their families. It took courage, determination, and hard work to survive, and ultimately thrive, in this environment.

Two settlements were quickly established, about 400 miles apart, on the southwestern part of the island. The settlements were known as the Eastern Settlement or Eystribyggð (present-day Qaqortoq) and the Western Settlement or Vestribyggð (close to the present-day capital of Nuuk). These settlements were not along the coast, as one might expect, but farther inland where the land was protected from the icy waters of the Arctic Sea and the cold foggy coastal weather. The Vikings were experienced farmers, and they knew how to identify the best land to settle in. No doubt Erik had scouted these locations during his exile and already earmarked the best land for himself.

Soon after the settlers arrived in Greenland, Erik was elected paramount chief of the Eastern Settlement. He was a strong leader, and he organized his followers to build homesteads and shelters before the onset of winter. Most built typical low, rectangular single-room Viking houses that they would have shared with their livestock, at least for the first winter until they had time to build barns. The only difference between the houses found in Greenland and those in other Scandinavian countries was that instead of using timber, the Greenlanders used stone as their primary building material. This would not have been by choice but rather through necessity. There were no great forests on Greenland, and stone was far more plentiful than timber.

Erik built a home for his family at a place he named Brattahlid, at the head of Eriksfjord approximately 96 km (60 miles) from the coast. But this was no single-room dwelling. As the paramount chief, Erik would have made sure he displayed his wealth and status. In Greenland his family lived liked jarls (nobles), and his home would certainly have had more than one room.

Once Erik settled on Greenland and became chief of the Eastern Settlement, he appeared to have put an end to his violent ways as there is no record of him committing any more crimes or murders. He settled into the life of a successful Viking farmer and trader, becoming wealthy and powerful. He still made numerous voyages to Iceland and even Norway, but he never again went on any more voyages of discovery. Under Erik's leadership, the Greenland settlement grew and flourished, and before long more immigrants braved the icy Atlantic and made the treacherous voyage from Iceland. Records indicate that Erik the Red died around 1002 during an epidemic that a group of new settlers bought to the island. His son, Leif Erikson, became chief of the Eastern settlement after Erik's death.

[1] *It is important to give credit where credit is due and mention that Erik the Red was actually not the first European to discover the landmass he named Greenland. That honor should most likely go to an Icelandic settler named Gunnbjorn Ulfsson. While sailing to Iceland, Ulfsson was blown off course during a storm and saw the shores of Greenland. However, he did not make landfall on the island but instead continued on his voyage. Erik may not have discovered Greenland, but he was most certainly the first European to create a permanent settlement on this remote island.*

[2] *There are two types of mirages, the inferior mirage and the superior mirage. The names do not refer to the size of the mirage, but rather to the deceptive position of an image relative to an object's actual position. The hillingar effect (also known as an artic mirage) is a superior mirage and describes an optical illusion or displacement of an observed image in an upward direction, thereby enabling a person to see beyond the horizon. Mirages are caused when light passes through layers of air of differing densities and the air refracts or bends the light. Superior*

mirages are most common in the Polar Regions and form when the ground or water surface is significantly colder than the air above it, and the temperature inversion refracts the light towards the colder air, making objects visible above their geographic position. Mirages trick the brain into thinking it is seeing something that isn't in fact really there or is different from what the brain is interpreting.

Chapter Fourteen: Leif Erikson – The First European to Land on the Shores of North America

Leif Erikson is another significant figure in Viking history. Like his father, Erik the Red, he was a great explorer and he is possibly the most famous figure in Norse history. Leif was the first European to set foot in North America, beating Christopher Columbus to the shores of this vast continent by almost half a millenium. But he not only changed the face of his world by discovering and exploring new territories, he also changed the land he lived in by converting the Greenlanders to Christianity.

Leif Erikson was the second son of Erik the Red, and he was born in Iceland before his father fell out with his neighbors. Leif later moved to Greenland with his family when Erik the Red founded the settlement there. By the time they arrived in Greenland, Leif was old enough to do his share of the work, and he would have toiled alongside the men to build homesteads for the families and shelters for the livestock. He experienced firsthand what it took to settle a harsh and inhospitable land.

This early introduction to settling a territory and the knowledge he gained working alongside his father would undoubtedly have stood Leif in good stead when he later landed on the shores of North America. He would have known how to choose a suitable site for settlement and what tasks needed to be completed to establish a base camp for the winter.

Erik also taught his son about ocean crossings and navigation, and apparently Leif had a natural aptitude for sailing. He developed quite the reputation as a seafarer. One legend tells how Leif, when he was about sixteen years old, spotted a polar bear on an ice floe and decided to hunt the bear. He used his knowledge of the sea and currents to take his boat upstream from the bear and let the current carry him to the ice floe; then he used the same method to get back to land. The people watching from the shore were suitably impressed by this tactic. There is no way of verifying the truth behind this story, but it is a good illustration of Leif's understanding of the sea and its currents, and of his natural talent as a sailor. Sailing and navigation were, after all, an integral part of Viking life, and these were skills that he likely shared with many of his fellow Vikings.

By the age of 24, Leif was ready to captain his first voyage, and around 997 he sailed to Norway, with a crew of fourteen men. At the time, it was not unusual for young men to serve as retainers in the household of a king or chief. This was an opportunity for Leif to forge alliances that would gain him status and political influence. When he arrived in Norway, Leif was welcomed to the court of King Olaf, where he spent the winter.

The time that Leif spent with King Olaf had a profound effect on the young man, and it was this king that converted Leif to Christianity. Until that time, Leif, like the rest of his family and the other settlers in Greenland, worshiped pagan Norse gods. In order to spread Christianity to the distant shores of Greenland, King Olaf needed a convert with influence in the settlements, and in Leif he found just such a person. When Leif left Norway, King Olaf gave him the task of spreading Christianity to Greenland.

Leif clearly took his mission from King Olaf seriously, but he wasn't yet ready to settle down to a life of farming in Greenland. Shortly after he returned from Norway, Leif began preparing for another voyage, one that would ultimately cement his place in history.

For many years, historians believed that the first European to set foot on the North American continent was Christopher Columbus, the Italian explorer, navigator, and colonizer, who landed there in 1492. While the contribution that this great European explorer made to history cannot be underestimated, it is now widely acknowledged that he was not the first European to discover the continent. That honor has been placed squarely on the broad shoulders of Leif Erikson, and today few historians dispute the fact that he beat Columbus to North America by almost 500 years.

Leif undertook this mammoth voyage shortly after his return from Norway. It is uncertain how long it took Leif and his crew of 35 men to sail across the Atlantic, but the *Saga of the Greenlanders*[1] claims that they made landfall at three different sites on the North American continent; they named these places, Helluland, Markland, and Vinland. There is still much debate as to exactly where each site was. The first place that they are believed to have landed was an icy and inhospitable region Erikson named Helluland. Helluland means "Land of the Stones" or "Flat-Stone Land," and many historians now believe that this was most likely Baffin Island. From there they sailed on until they came to a heavily forested stretch of coastline that they called "Markland." Markland means "Wood Land," and this could be Labrador. They did not, however, choose to establish any sort of settlement there and sailed farther south along the coast, quite possibly looking for a more suitable place to build a base camp. Approximately two days later, they came to a headland with an island just offshore. This appeared to be a more hospitable area than Helluland and Markland, and Leif decided to build his camp there and named the area Vinland, most likely due to the abundance of wild grapes they found in the region. The exact location of Vinland remains controversial and it could have been as far north as Newfoundland or as far south as Cape Cod.

Leif only undertook one voyage to Vinland, and after he returned to Greenland, he never made any more voyages of discovery. The exact reason for this is unknown, but it could be related to the death of his father, Erik the Red. History is unclear about where exactly Leif was when his father died; some accounts say that he only returned to Greenland after Erik's death, while others speculate that Erik died shortly after Leif returned from Vinland. Either way, after Erik's death, Leif took over as chief of the Eastern Settlement and remained at Brattahlid until his death some 20 years later. During his time as chief, Leif used his power and influence to convert many of the Greenlanders to the Christian faith.

After Leif's death, his son, Thorkel Leifson, became the next chief. After that, the family of Erik the Red fades into obscurity. This is mostly due to the lack of any surviving historical records from the Greenland settlement. If there are any living descendants of Erik the Red and Leif Erikson, they are most likely to be found in modern-day Scandinavia or perhaps even North America.

Unfortunately, due to the lack of accurate historical records and limited archaeological finds, the impact that Leif Erikson had on world history can never be truly quantified. This mighty Norseman had the courage and vision to leave the safe shores of his homeland and discover America almost half a century before Christopher Columbus, and he did it in an open Viking longboat. This took remarkable seafaring ability and navigational skills. He redefined the boundaries of the Viking world and his successful voyage to Vinland encouraged others to follow in his footsteps and visit the North American continent. Contact with the local tribes would have undoubtedly had a lasting effect on both cultures. This extraordinary man rightly deserves his place in history as a renowned explorer and the first European to set foot on the North American continent.

[1] Grœnlendinga saga - The Saga of the Greenlanders
(https://notendur.hi.is/haukurth/utgafa/greenlanders.html)

Chapter Fifteen: The Sagas

Much has been written about Leif and his remarkable voyage across the Atlantic, but unfortunately no historical records exist from his lifetime. Most accounts of the discovery and attempted settlement of Vinland are based on two Icelandic sagas, namely the *Saga of Erik the Red* and the *Saga of the Greenlanders*, written in Iceland approximately 250 years after the events they describe. Leif's story has been embellished, diminished, and altered over time, depending on the motivations of the writer. While both sagas refer to Leif Erikson and his voyage to the North American continent and contain similar elements, they also differ greatly. Here is a brief summary of the two sagas.

The Saga of the Greenlanders (Groenlendinga Saga)[1]

The *Saga of the Greenlanders* not only describes Leif's voyage to Vinland but also subsequent voyages to the new land. According to the *Saga of the Greenlanders*, Leif's voyage to Vinland was planned and deliberate. The saga describes how Leif knew about the existence of North America because an Icelandic adventurer, Bjarni Herjolfsson had accidentally discovered a new land to the west of

Greenland in about 986; in this version of the discovery of Vinland, Bjarni does not go ashore. He sees the landmass from his boat, but when he realizes it cannot possibly be Greenland because there are no glaciers and ice floes, he sails on without making landfall. When Bjarni finally reaches Greenland, he settles on his father's farm and there he remained. He never attempts to mount an expedition to return to the mysterious land that he had seen. He does, however, tell his story to other settlers on Greenland, and this ultimately inspires Leif Erikson, some fifteen years later, to organize an expedition to explore this land. In the *Saga of the Greenlanders*, Leif is the main explorer of Vinland, and he establishes a base camp at Leifsbudir. This serves as a boat repair station, storage area for timber and grapes before they are shipped to Greenland, and a base for subsequent expeditions. Leif retraces Bjarni's route in reverse, past Helluland (land of flat stone) and Markland (land of forests) before sailing across the open sea for another two days until he finds a headland with an island just offshore and a pool accessible to ships at high tide. Leif and his crew make landfall in the area and establish a base. They name the area Vinland, and the winter is described as mild rather than freezing. It is here that they are reputed to have found an abundance of wild grapes. In the spring, Leif returns to Greenland with a boatload of timber and grapes, never to return to Vinland again. The second expedition to Vinland is led by Leif's older brother, Thorvald, with a crew of about 40 men. This group spends three winters at the base that Leif had established, Leifsbudir. They explore the west coast of the new land in the first summer and the east coast in the second summer. During their exploration of Vinland, they establish contact with the local inhabitants that they called Skraelings. At first, their meetings are peaceful, but slowly animosity and mistrust grow between the two groups and later violence breaks out. After killing some Skraelings, the Norse explorers are attacked by a large force of them, and Thorvald is fatally wounded by an arrow, becoming the first European to die on North American soil. The following spring the remaining Greenlanders decide to return home. Leif's younger brother,

Thorstein, leads a third expedition to Vinland to recover Thorvald's body, but he is driven off course and spends the summer wandering aimlessly in the Atlantic before returning to Greenland, having failed in his mission. The following winter Thorstein dies from illness, and his widow, Gudrid, marries Thorfinn Karlsefni, an Icelander. Thorfinn agrees to lead another expedition to Vinland. This is a larger expedition, and Gudrid accompanies her husband; they even take livestock with them. Their intent appears to be to form a more permanent settlement in Vinland. Gudrid gives birth to a son, Snorri, in Vinland, but shortly after his birth, the group is attacked by the local inhabitants. However, they manage to retreat to a defensive position and are able to survive the attack. The following summer they return to Greenland with a cargo of grapes, timber, and hides. Shortly after this, Leif's sister, Freydis, persuades the captain of an Icelandic ship to mount an expedition to Vinland. They set sail in the autumn and spend the winter at Leif's camp, but disagreements between Freydis and the Icelandic captain leads to the killing of the captain and his Icelandic crew. The Greenlanders then return home with their cargo. This is the last Vinland expedition recorded in the *Saga of the Greenlanders*.

The Saga of Erik the Red (Eirik's Saga)[2]

In this version of the story, Leif accidentally discovers the North American continent on his return to Greenland following a visit to King Olaf Tryggvason in Norway. On his return voyage he is blown off course during a storm and makes landfall on a mysterious land where he spends the winter. On his return to Greenland, he brings with him not only the Christian religion but also a cargo of grapes, wheat, and timber. He also rescues survivors from a wrecked ship, which earns him the nickname Leif the Lucky. The *Saga of Erik the Red*, like the *Saga of the Greenlanders*, states that this was the only voyage that Leif made to Vinland. In the spring after Leif returned, his younger brother, Thorstein, leads the next expedition to the new land, but is driven off course by a storm and spends the entire summer wandering aimlessly in the Atlantic. He returns to

Greenland without ever making it to Vinland. On his return Thorstein marries Gudrid, but he dies of illness in the winter. The following winter Gudrid marries a visiting Icelander named Thorfinn Karlsefni. He agrees to undertake the largest expedition to Vinland. His wife accompanies him on this voyage, and they also take livestock with them. They are accompanied by another pair of Icelanders, Bjarni Grimolfsson and Thorhall Gamlason, as well as Leif's older brother, Thorvald, his sister, Freydis, and her husband, Thorvard. They sail past Helluland and Markland and continue past some extraordinarily long beaches before landing along the coast and sending out two scouts to explore the land. After three days, the scouts return with grapes and wheat. The expedition sails on until they come to an inlet with an island just offshore and there they make camp. This camp is called Straumfjord. The winter is apparently harsh, and food is scarce. When spring comes, Thorhall Gamlason wants to sail north to find Vinland, but Thorfinn Karlsefni wants to sail southwards. Thorhall takes nine men and sails north, but his vessel is swept out to sea and never seen again. Thorfinn and the rest sail down the east coast with approximately 40 men and establish a camp on the shore of a lagoon. The settlement was known as Hop, and there they found an abundance of wild grapes and wheat. How long they stayed there is unclear, but they did have contact with the local people. The initial encounters are peaceful, and the locals trade with the Norse on various occasions. One day, however, the local people become frightened by the Greenlander's bull and they attack the explorers. The Greenlanders manage to survive the attack by retreating to a more defensive position. After that, the explorers abandon their southern camp and sail north again. Karlsefni and Thorvald Eriksson take a crew and sail in search of Thorhall. They once again have a hostile encounter with the local people, and Thorvald is shot with an arrow and dies from his wound. The explorers remain on the continent for one more winter, but the situation is tense and there are disagreements amongst them. The following summer they abandon their venture and start the return voyage home to Greenland. This is the last Vinland expedition recorded in the *Saga of Erik the Red.*

A notable difference between the two sagas is that in the *Saga of Erik the Red*, Leif's role has been reduced to that of accidental discoverer of Vinland with Thorfinn Karlsefni as the main explorer of Vinland. Bjarni Herjolfsson's voyage fifteen years earlier is not mentioned at all. In the *Saga of the Greenlanders*, there are five attempted expeditions to Vinland over the course of a number of years, but in the *Saga of Erik the Red*, there is only one huge expedition after Leif discovers Vinland. The name Leifsbudir does not appear in the *Saga of Erik the Red*; instead two camps are mentioned, Straumfjord (Fjord of Currents) and Hop (Tidal Lagoon). Straumfjord is the main base where the explorers spend the winter, and Hop is the summer camp where timber is cut and grapes are collected and then shipped to Straumfjord before being taken to Greenland. The reason for the differences in the two sagas is unclear. Both were based on oral histories and written long after the actual events, so it could be as simple as two different interpretations with different authors placing different emphasis on different events. Bear in mind that both versions were written by Icelanders that might have had different agendas. The writer of the *Saga of Erik the Red* may have wanted to make the Icelanders' contribution to the discovery of Vinland the significant part of the story; therefore, Thorfinn Karlsefni's role is greatly embellished, and Leif Erikson is only mentioned briefly. The details of the two sagas may differ greatly, but the fundamental premise that Leif Erikson was the first European to land on the North American continent is common to both.

While these two examples deal primarily with the discovery of Vinland and Leif Erikson's role in this remarkable part of history, they also serve as a good illustration of how the history of the Vikings has been altered and interpreted over the centuries.

---

[1] Grœnlendinga saga - The Saga of the Greenlanders
(https://notendur.hi.is/haukurth/utgafa/greenlanders.html)

[2] The Saga of Erik the Red 1880 translation into English by J. Sephton from the original Icelandic 'Eiríks saga rauða' (http://sagadb.org/files/pdf/eiriks_saga_rauda.en.pdf)

Chapter Sixteen: The Significance of the Settlement of Iceland, Greenland, and Vinland

For many Viking enthusiasts drawn to their legacy of warmongering and violence, the settlements of Iceland and Greenland, and the discovery of Vinland, may seem like an aside to the story of these great warriors, but this is actually a very significant part of Viking history and should not be overshadowed by their exploits on the battlefield.

The settlements of Iceland and Greenland clearly illustrate that the Vikings were not just opportunistic attackers who launched blitz hit-and-run raids on unsuspecting communities before disappearing into the mist. They also had the tenacity and ability to cross the open ocean, braving rough seas and foul weather, to establish successful settlements in far-flung territories.

The first Norsemen reached Iceland around 860, and a man called Floki Vilgeroarson was so dismayed by the harshness of the climate that he named the frozen, snow-covered island Iceland. But prospective settlers were not deterred by the name, and the first wave of Norsemen began moving to Iceland during the 870s and established a very successful colony on the island that exists to this day.

The first Viking settlers in Iceland came predominantly from the area around Bergen in Norway. Their main reason for leaving Bergen was most likely to escape the draconian rule of King Harald Fairhair. Other early settlers in Iceland also came from various parts of Scandinavia and even from the British Isles (a number of Celts probably came with the Vikings as spouses and slaves). By the middle of the 10th century, Iceland had thousands of inhabitants. From Iceland, the Vikings migrated to Greenland.

Here once again they were able to establish a successful colony, providing further evidence of their tenacity and ability to build settlements from the ground up. The settlement in Greenland allowed the Vikings to hunt and fish as far north as Disko Bay, above the Arctic Circle, keeping Europe well supplied with furs and skins, and introducing them to exotic items like narwhal tusks, sold as "unicorn horns." This trade with Europe increased the overall wealth of Norway, but it also enabled Vikings, who may not have had many prospects in their homelands, to become powerful and wealthy. In Greenland, ordinary men, like Erik the Red, were able to own large tracts of land and live like jarls, something that would not have been possible for them in Scandinavia where land was becoming scarce. The settlement of Iceland and Greenland enabled many Vikings to flee the tyrannical rule of unpopular monarchs and free themselves from a life of oppression.

One of the most significant contributions the settlement of Greenland made to broader world history is that it was a stepping stone to the European discovery of the American continent. Without the colony on Greenland, the Vikings never would have made the voyage to North America; it would just not have been physically possible. Greenland provided the physical starting point and launch pad for Leif's incredible voyage. Once the Vikings had settled in Greenland, it was only a matter of time before they reached the shores of North America. The shortest distance between Greenland

and Canada is the Davis Strait, and here the two landmasses are only separated by 250 nautical miles. For seafarers accustomed to making the 1,500 nautical mile crossing between Norway and Greenland, this relatively short distance would not have presented much of a challenge. Viking explorers were already used to living in freezing conditions and dealing with rough waters, frozen seas, ice floes, and the various other challenges of sailing in the open ocean, so they would naturally have attempted the Atlantic crossing. If Leif had lived anywhere else in the world at the time, he probably never would have been the first European to visit North America.

The settlement of Iceland and Greenland, and the attempted settlement of Vinland, has provided scholars and historians with great insight into Viking culture and society. Artifacts found at abandoned Viking settlements in Greenland and Vinland illustrate how far the Vikings were able to travel in their longboats and demonstrate their willingness and ability to settle in harsh and inhospitable lands.

Chapter Seventeen: The Decline of Vinland

The discovery of North America by the Vikings is a significant milestone in world history, but the Norsemen did not stay long on this continent. For modern Americans, it may seem strange that the Greenlanders decided so quickly to abandon any attempts at a permanent settlement in Vinland. On the surface, the continent appeared to offer the Norsemen everything they were looking for. It was certainly a far more hospitable environment than Greenland, the climate was moderate, grazing was plentiful, and the land was fertile. And, of course, there were large forests and plenty of wood for building homesteads and ships. So why didn't the Vikings settle in Vinland?

The main reason appears to be that it was just not economically viable. During the Viking Age, Vinland actually had very little to offer the Greenlanders in comparison to Europe. The resources available in Vinland, mostly grapes and timber, were not enough to make the treacherous voyage worthwhile. The distance between Greenland and Vinland was almost 3,500 km (2,100 miles), and the same commodities were available in Norway. Europe was also a source of luxury goods, like spices from the East, salt, textiles, glass, and other commodities that the Greenlanders could not find in Vinland or produce for themselves.

Regular voyages between Greenland, Iceland, and Norway were also essential to ensure the political and cultural survival of the island. The settlers viewed themselves as Norse and followed their Norse traditions. When they moved to Iceland and Greenland, they were not looking to establish new independent homelands or break ties with Norway. Many would have retained their contacts and political connections in their old homeland. If the Vikings had established a settlement in Vinland, it would have been a satellite colony, and that was not just viable; Vinland was just too far away to be an efficient and cost-effective Viking settlement.

The size of the colony on Greenland also made the settlement of Vinland impractical. The small and newly established colony of Greenland could not afford to send 30 or 40 of their most able-bodied men to Vinland for three or four years at a time. They needed those men to help establish and maintain farms and homesteads on the island. When Erik decided to leave Iceland and start a settlement on Greenland, there were various reasons for others to follow him. But at the time of Leif's voyage to Vinland, Greenland was still a relatively new settlement and there were still plenty of resources for all the settlers.

Another disadvantage of colonizing Vinland was that, unlike Greenland, the North American continent was already inhabited by a large indigenous population. There was some trade between the Vikings and the local tribes, but there were also hostile encounters. The number of settlers was relatively small, and they were always vulnerable to attack.

The discovery of the North American continent was an amazing achievement for the Vikings. It cemented their place in history as great seafarers and explorers, and ensured that Leif Erikson will never be forgotten. Unfortunately, a combination of factors meant that from the time of Leif's voyage to Vinland and the eventual abandonment of any kind of settlement on the North American continent was less than ten years. And it would take another half a century before Europeans again tried to settle on the continent.

Chapter Eighteen: The Decline of the Greenland Colony

The founding of the colony in Greenland was probably Erik the Red's greatest contribution to world history and his most enduring legacy. It certainly earned him his place in the Old Icelandic sagas and in the modern history books, but unfortunately, Erik's colony was not able to survive for as long as his story has endured. For half a century, there were Norsemen living in Greenland, and at the height of the colony's existence, the Viking population numbered between 3,000 and 5,000 inhabitants living on 300 to 400 farms. Greenland was more than a mere outpost; it was a well-established settlement where the majority of Greenlanders spent their entire lives and for the most part, we assume, were happy.

Even though these people always considered themselves Norse and retained strong ties with Norway and Iceland, they were for all intents and purposes Greenlanders. For many, this was the only land they ever knew. It is where they were born, raised, married, had families, and eventually died. Many made successful lives for themselves in this icy and often harsh environment. But unfortunately, the Norse population of Greenland did not survive into the modern age. The land that Erik the Red and his followers struggled so hard to tame could sadly not support their descendants forever.

Survival on Greenland was almost entirely dependent on natural resources, and eventually life became too hard for those living in this harsh environment. Approximately 500 years after Erik had explored Greenland and decided to make it his home, both the Eastern and Western Settlements had been abandoned. Theories and speculations abound as to why life on the island became unsustainable, forcing the Norse to eventually abandon it, but the exact reasons remain unknown. Perhaps one day, through historical research and archeological finds, the answers may reveal themselves, but for now the island has yet to give up all its secrets. What is known is that sometime between the 15th and 17th centuries the entire Norse population of Greenland vanished.

From the start of the colony, Greenland's economy was based on farming, fishing, hunting, and trade. The sea around the island was teeming with life, and during the summer each settlement sent men to hunt in Disko Bay above the Arctic Circle. They returned with meat that could be dried and eaten during the long winter months when fresh food was scarce, along with other valuable commodities such as seal pelts and walrus tusks that could be traded and sold to Icelandic traders or on trading voyages to Norway. It was primarily this trade between Greenland and Norway that enabled the colony to survive and the settlers to buy much-needed resources, such as timber for homesteads and shipbuilding, which were not readily available on the island.

Most historians agree that it is unlikely that one single catastrophic event destroyed the settlement. It is far more likely that a combination of factors led to the demise of both Viking settlements and eventually forced the Greenlanders to abandon their lifelong homes and move to other more hospitable and sustainable regions.

The Little Ice Age, a period during which Europe and North America experienced unnaturally cold, harsh winters, could have contributed to the decline of the settlement. As a result of these harsh conditions, crops would have failed, and this would have been followed by widespread famine throughout the region. Everyday life would have been extremely hard, and farming on Greenland would have become more and more difficult. As grazing on the island became sparse, there is archeological evidence that they shifted their focus from large cattle to smaller livestock such as sheep and goats. This alone would not have driven the Greenlanders from their homeland. They would still have been able to survive by shifting their focus from farming to fishing, seal hunting, and fur trading,

During the Viking Age, Greenland's biggest exports were walrus tusks, seal pelts, and so-called "unicorn horns." At the time, most Scandinavians wore clothes made of skins, homespun wool, and furs, so there was always a market for the polar bear furs, seal pelts, wool, arctic fox furs, and caribou skins that the Greenlanders had almost unlimited access to. They also exported luxuries, such as walrus tusks and unicorn horns, to the royal courts of Europe. Obviously, there were no actual unicorns in Greenland, but the Vikings appeared to have been clever marketers and knew how to sell their products. The so-called "unicorn horn" was actually the tusk of the narwhal, a whale found only in the icy waters of the northernmost oceans. Narwhals are relatively small, and the males have a left canine that twists in a spiral and can grow up to ten feet long. For a time, these tusks were highly prized by the Europeans. They crushed the horns for medicinal purposes, and in the French court, the king's food was served in unicorn horns. However, as fashion and tastes on the European continent changed, there would have been less demand for the natural resources that the Greenlanders relied on so heavily as part of their trade with Europe. As furs, skins, and unicorn horns declined in popularity, so did the economy of the island.

Unfortunately for the Greenlanders, not only were the products they produced no longer in great demand, trade routes were also changing. The decline of the settlement coincided with Christopher

Columbus' voyage to the Americas, and it was highly likely that the world was just changing. With new territories to explore and trade opportunities opening up in the west, Europeans probably no longer had a use for Greenland. The cold, icy landmass to the north no longer held any fascination for Europeans as they now turned their attention to the Americas and everything that the vast, unexplored continent had to offer.

Growing isolation would also have contributed to the decline and eventual demise of the Norse settlement. Ship traffic between Iceland and Norway was becoming more sporadic. While shipbuilding may have improved in the half a century since Erik the Red founded Greenland; the sea remained treacherous, especially so far north. Icebergs and giant waves were a constant danger in the frigid waters, and with the dwindling demand for resources and products from Greenland, fewer traders were willing to make the long and arduous voyage. In the same way that it had not been worth the Greenlanders' efforts to travel regularly to Vinland for resources, it was no longer economically viable for traders to make the voyage to Greenland. As a result, not only was it more difficult for the Greenlanders to sell their produce, supplies to the colony also became more sporadic and expensive.

Increasing isolation also meant that the Greenlanders were losing touch with their national identity and Norse heritage. Without regular trade and travel to Norway, the Greenlanders were becoming more and more isolated from their homeland and culture, and this would have impacted the mental health of the colony. They may have suffered from depression and lacked the motivation to keep the colony moving forward. The world around them was changing, and Greenland was being left behind. The colony no longer offered many opportunities for younger generations. There was no more arable land available for younger sons, and due to the change in climate, the land that was available was becoming more marginal for farming, meaning there was less grazing for livestock.

The abandonment of Greenland appears to have taken place in an orderly manner. This also suggests that the colony declined slowly rather than being abandoned suddenly as a result of one cataclysmic event. Excavations on the island have turned up very few valuables, and archeologists believe this indicates that the settlers left in an orderly fashion and took everything of value with them. Besides not knowing why the Greenlanders left, there are also no records of where they went. For the most part, they were most likely assimilated back into Norwegian society. Having kept close ties with Norway for most of the time that the colony existed and because there were no indigenous people on Greenland to influence the Norse culture, the Greenlanders would have retained their Norse identity and could still relate to the Norwegian way of life. This would have made it possible for them to return to Norway and easily adapt to the environment.

Strong, able-bodied Greenlanders of child-bearing age would have been the first to abandon life on the island. They would have left their childhood homes and families to seek opportunities elsewhere. In the same way that Erik and his followers came to Greenland looking for a better life, the more adventurous Greenlanders were later forced to leave the island to make a better life for themselves. Erik the Red would probably have been sad to see his descendants dispersed and his colony abandoned, but he would surely have admired the tenacity and spirit of the Greenlanders who, like him, were not afraid to leave their homeland and build new lives elsewhere.

Timeline for the Viking Age of Exploration

The exact dates of the major milestones are not recorded, but a timeline can be drawn up that approximates the most important dates.

Circa 860 – The first Norsemen reach Iceland

Circa 870 – A Norse colony is established on Iceland

Between 950 and 960 - Erik Thorvaldsson, better known by his nickname Erik the Red, is born in Rogaland on the southwestern coast of Norway. He is the son of Thorvald Asvaldsson.

Circa 960 - Thorvald Asvaldsson commits murder and is banished from Norway. He takes his family to Iceland and settles in Hornstrandir.

Circa 970 - Erik the Red's second son, Leif Erikson, is born in Iceland

Circa 980 - Erik the Red fights with his neighbors and is convicted of killing Eyiolf the Foul. He is banished from Haukadal and moves further north to Oxney with his family. **Circa 982** - Erik is again found guilty of killing his fellow Norsemen and is banned from Iceland for three years

982 to 985 - Erik and his crew explore Greenland

Circa 985 - Erik returns to Iceland

Summer 986 - Erik the Red sets sail with 25 ships and approximately 300 followers to establish a settlement on Greenland. Only 14 ships survive the voyage. The Vikings form two settlements in Greenland.

Circa 999 – Erik's son, Leif Erikson, sails to Norway. In Norway, Leif Erikson spends the winter in the household of King Olaf Tryggvason and is converted to Christianity.

Circa 1000 –Leif Erikson returns to Greenland, but soon afterward, he takes a small group of Vikings and sets sail on a voyage of discovery to the North American continent. Leif and his crew establish a small settlement in an area that he calls Vinland, which historians believe could be modern-day Newfoundland.

Circa 1002 – Erik the Red dies in Greenland during an epidemic

Circa 1003 – Leif leaves the settlement at Vinland and returns to his father's estate at Brattahlid in Greenland. He becomes chief of the Eastern Settlement and never returns to Vinland.

Between 1004 and 1010 – The Greenlanders make more voyages to Vinland. Erik the Red's son, Thorvald, is killed by the local inhabitants in North America and is the first European to die on the continent.

Circa 1010 – The settlement at Vinland declines and fails mainly due to attacks from indigenous tribes and unsustainability

Circa 1025 – Erik's son, Leif Erikson, dies and his grandson, Thorkel Leifson, becomes chief of the Eastern Settlement

Between the 15th and 17th Century – The Norse settlements in Greenland decline and are eventually abandoned

Chapter Nineteen: Viking Society and Everyday Life

The Vikings were not just a bunch of hooligans running amok in Europe, raiding and plundering. They were part of a complex and well-ordered society. The average Norseman spent most of his life farming, trading, or working as a craftsman. The men were blacksmiths, fur traders, hunters, farmers, fishermen, and shipbuilders. They worked the land and grew crops such as wheat, barley, and rye, and tended to their livestock.

Norse society had three tiers. On the top were jarls, who were wealthy men who owned property and ships. Early in the Viking Age, there were no national kings but rather many chieftains who controlled smaller areas. As the Viking Age progressed, power became centralized in the hands of a few strong leaders, and they became the kings of Sweden, Norway, and Denmark in the 9th century. As these kings rose to power in Scandinavia, the jarls became aristocrats who were subordinate to the kings and held land for them at their pleasure. In peacetime, the jarls oversaw the management of their own lands, and during war or on raiding expeditions they commanded the longboat crews. Jarls also protected the honor, prosperity, and security of their followers, and in return, their followers supported them, went on raids, and followed their jarl into battle.

Like the jarls, the kings were also drawn from the nobility or ruling class. In Norse society, the king was not viewed as special or divine, and the position of king was not necessarily guaranteed through succession. A son could inherit his father's throne, but it was not a given. Norse kings were expected to be strong, brave, generous, and fearless in battle. A weak or unpopular monarch could be replaced by a rebellion or an election if the jarls united behind a rival claimant. If the king was not strong enough to ensure the loyalty of the jarls, then he would be replaced. In this way, a jarl might become strong and rich enough to make himself a king, but he could also move down the ranks and become a karl if he lost his fortune. Odin was the principal god of the upper classes, and they would strive to emulate his wisdom, vast knowledge, and creative spark.[1]

The next rung in Viking society were the karls. The karls, or Norse middle class, were farmers, fishermen, and craftsmen. On raiding expeditions or during war, they were the rank and file of the Viking army and they crewed the longboats. Many young karls went on raiding expeditions to increase their wealth so that they could buy land and perhaps even increase their social standing. In some cases, they even became jarls. Inheritance customs in the Viking world typically meant that the older son would inherit most of his father's fortune. This meant that Viking raiders were frequently ambitious younger sons who hadn't inherited much and were dissatisfied with their lot in their home countries.[2] These Viking warriors aspired to as brave as Thor, the principle deity of the middle classes.[3] There was a subclass of karls, known as kuskarls (house karls). They served as the personal staff or bodyguards of a jarl or king.

Jarls and karls were free men, but the third strata of Norse society, the thralls, were little more than slaves. This group was predominantly made up of convicted criminals, captives from raiding expeditions, or prisoners of war. Slave trading was still common practice throughout Europe and the Middle East, and many

Vikings made their fortunes in the slave trade. They captured young men and women during raids and sold them in the slave markets across Europe. Some thralls were also born into slavery, as the children of thralls were automatically thralls themselves. Thralls had no rights, and the killing of a thrall was considered destruction of property rather than murder. Viking raiders bought and sold slaves and captives from parts of Europe, Britain, and the Middle East, and this meant that the thralls were not one ethnic or cultural group.

Poor Norsemen or women could also become slaves by giving up their freedom in order to pay off their debts. In the same way that a free person could sell themselves into slavery, a thrall could also buy their way out of slavery by selling handicrafts made during their free time. A thrall might move up in society to become a karl, but it is unlikely that they would progress further than that.

A Norseman's position in society was not cast in stone, and as illustrated above, a man could, to some degree, move up and down in Norse society. There were also richer and poorer men in each stratum. Norse women usually had the same status in society as their fathers or husbands and, unlike their counterparts in Christian Europe, could own land and conduct businesses in their own right.

The rule of law, fairness, and justice was extremely important to the Vikings. They had no centralized government but well-established laws formed the root of their society and they lived in orderly, structured communities. Each small settlement had their own chief. The chief, however, was not all-powerful, and decisions regarding village life were made collectively at a meeting called the "Thing." The Thing was a public gathering that could be held at any time which gave all freemen in the settlement the opportunity to settle disputes and express their views on certain village matters. The Thing is comparable to a modern-day legislative assembly.

The chief of the settlement ran the Thing, but he and his council could only guide proceedings, as all the freemen in the settlement had the right to take part in the decision-making process. During the

Thing, the members of the settlement voted on day-to-day issues, including who owned a portion of land or what punishment an offender would receive if they were found guilty of breaking the law. Once a year the freemen of a settlement gathered for the "Althing." This was an annual event where new laws were made and the Vikings could vote on important decisions like taxes, peace treaties, and, if necessary, the election of a new chief or king.

The Thing could be called to enforce the law and try men accused of committing crimes. During the Thing, the accused could defend themselves and call witnesses. The rule of law was important to maintain order in the harsh and often violent Viking settlements so punishments could be severe. The ultimate punishment for violent crimes was usually to outlaw, or banish, the guilty. Depending on the crime, the banishment could be permanent or for a set number of years.

Outlaws were forced to flee their villages and hide in the wilderness. Once a Viking was declared an outlaw, anyone was allowed to hunt them down and kill them. Outlaws could also be stripped of all their worldly possessions and property. If a Viking was only outlawed for a predetermined amount of time, they were usually allowed to keep their possessions and return to their homes when their banishment was lifted.

Lesser crimes could be settled by a duel, known as a holmgang. This did not always end well for the victim and justice was not necessarily on the right side, but since the Vikings believed the gods favored the righteous, the outcome was seen to be fair. Land could also be confiscated from the guilty and given to the victim, or the guilty might had to pay compensation to the victim's family. Money paid to a family of the victim was known as wergild.[4]

One person in every settlement was assigned the duty of law-speaker. This was a very important position because during the early Viking Age there were no law books or written laws. Even though all settlements held their own annual Althing and made their own laws, some laws applied to all Vikings, and the law-speaker had to memorize them all. He had to know the laws of the settlement and those of broader Viking society. If there was any confusion about a law during the Thing or the Althing, the law-speaker would be called upon to explain it. Every Viking settlement had a law-rock, and after new laws were passed, the law-speaker had to go to the law-rock and recite all the laws so that the women, children, and slaves who were not permitted to be present at the Althing would also know the laws.

Every member of the family, from toddler to grandparent, was expected to pull their weight. Boys worked alongside their fathers, plowing land and planting and harvesting crops. Women and girls took care of the family, raised the children, made the clothes, and cooked the meals. Viking food was basic and they had to make do with what they could grow themselves or gather from the surrounding area. Their diet consisted mainly of bread, porridge, cabbage, onions, leeks, and wild berries. They grew crops such as barley, rye, oats, and a variety of vegetables, while cows, sheep, and goats all provided milk, cheese, and butter. While to some modern people, this subsistence lifestyle may sound like some kind of romantic idyll, it was anything but. It was a hard, perilous existence where daily life was often a grueling struggle for survival.

While Viking society was patriarchal, women were seen as valued members of the community and their contribution to Viking life was just as important as that of the men. When the men were away hunting, fishing, trading, or raiding, the women were left in charge of the farms and the households. It then became solely their responsibility to care for the family and oversee all the farm work. They had to ensure that when the men returned the farm was running smoothly. Women also traveled with and worked alongside their husbands to establish new colonies in Iceland and Greenland. Viking women certainly had more power than most European women at the time. They could divorce their husbands, own property, and participate in trade. This enabled some of them to become wealthy in their own right. Viking woman may have had more rights than their

European counterparts, but their main task was still that of homemaker.

The homes of the Vikings were rather basic. Vikings lived in single-roomed, low rectangular-shaped dwellings. The interior of a Norse house was plain and basic. A single room, with a reed or flagstone floor, served as both the living and sleeping area for the average Viking family. Damp rose up through the rough walls while the wind whistled through the small openings that served as windows. The smoke from the central cooking hearth swirled around the dark interior of the dwelling before escaping out of a hole in the reed roof. The lodgings may have provided shelter from the harsh weather, but there were few comforts. There would have been a table and a few stools where meals were eaten and rug-covered benches along the walls that served as beds. A wealthier Viking's dwelling may have had what were considered a few more luxuries, but it certainly wouldn't have been grand or lavish by today's standards. A wealthier family's house would have had more than one room, perhaps a few tapestries hanging on the wall, and the family probably slept on straw-stuffed mattresses rather than hard benches. But their houses were still dark, damp, and smoky.

Fortunately, the life of a Viking was not all fighting, work, and drudgery. There was also time for sports and other entertainment. The Vikings enjoyed wrestling, ice-skating, skiing, archery, and falconry. They demonstrated their strength with stone-lifting competitions and enjoyed a game called knattleikr that involved a ball, full-body contact, and at times a bat. These games would surely have provided a welcome respite from working the lands and caring for the livestock. But the games, which were often violent and could result in serious injury or even death, were not just pure entertainment; they also allowed the men to practice vital battle skills and improve their fighting techniques. The games also enabled young boys to learn the skills that they would need to be great Viking warriors and to demonstrate their strength, agility, and battle tactics.

During the long, harsh winters, Norsemen were accustomed to spending much of their time indoors, and board games were a popular pastime. They amused themselves playing dice, chess, and board games like Hnefatafl and Kvatrutafl. Kvatrutafl was a game similar to backgammon, and Hnefatafl was a type of war game that is thought to have helped teach players battle strategies. The Norsemen also enjoyed listening to stories, telling riddles, and playing musical instruments such as harps, horns, and pipes.

Storytelling and the reciting of sagas, especially those about the exploits of Viking heroes, were deeply ingrained in Norse society. During Viking feasts, Scandinavian bards, called skalds, recited epic poems or sagas that praised the brave deeds of Viking warriors and their prowess in battle. These sagas were important to the Vikings because, before they converted to Christianity, they had no written records of significant events, and their history was passed on through the sagas told by the skalds. This was their only way of preserving their history, so these sagas were often incredibly long and detailed. Some, like the *Saga of Erik the Red* and the *Saga of the Greenlanders*, were eventually written down, but not until long after the events that they describe. Unfortunately, many more were lost to history.

[1] Davis, Graeme; The Cult of Thor (All About History, Issue 057, p35)

[2] Winroth, Anders. 2014. The Age of the Vikings. p. 164-165

[3] Wilson, David M. 1989. The Vikings and Their Origins. p. 114-115

[4] D.J. Williamson et al; The Rules of Revenge; Viking Justice (All About History, Issue 059) p 29 – 33

Chapter Twenty: Pagan Gods and Norse Mythology

Norse paganism was not a monotheistic religion. In Norse mythology, there were various spiritual beings, including gods, goddesses, giants, elves, dwarves, spirits, and other powerful creatures that influenced the lives of men. There were also various worlds in which all these different beings dwelled.

Asgard, a large fortified castle that floated in the air, was the home of the gods. The gods and goddesses most venerated by the Vikings were Odin, Thor, Loki, Baldur, Frigg, Freya, Freyr, and Njoror. Odin was the ruler of the deities, a powerful war god and seeker of wisdom. He was also the father of Thor who with his magic hammer, Mjolnir, protected mankind and the realm of Midgard where humans lived. Thor was also worshiped as the god of warriors, and Vikings tried to emulate his courage in battle. Loki was a dangerous and mischievous half-god, half-giant who wreaked havoc among the other gods.

Jotunheim, found at the edge of the world, was the home of the giants who caused chaos and destruction throughout the world. The giants were related to the gods but were also their enemies. In Norse legend, Thor hunts giants in order to protect mankind from their chaos and destruction. Besides the gods who lived in the air, and the giants who lived in the world, there were also dwarves who lived underground in Svartalfheim. They were the miners and smiths of the mythological world, but they were not short humans as people tend to imagine, but rather powerful, invisible spiritual beings. The Norsemen also believed in elves, who were demi-gods and land spirits who inhabited everything on land. These land spirits had considerable power over the land and all those who dwelled in it.

As seafarers, one of the gods that they constantly sought to appease was Aegir. As the commander of the sea, Aegir was loved and feared in equal measure by the seafaring Vikings. According to Norse legends, Aegir and his wife, Ran, dwelled in a magnificent feast hall beneath the ocean, with Ran often depicted as drowning unfortunate sailors. When a Norse ship sank, it was believed that the dead sailors would forever dine in Aegir's Hall.

The Vikings actually had a complicated view of the afterlife. Unlike popular culture has led us to believe, they did not simply think that all warriors who died in battle would reside in Valhalla, the Hall of the Fallen and realm of the god Odin, for eternity. There was, in fact, more than one Land of the Dead in Viking pagan religion.

Unfortunately, Norse mythology is not clear on how a person ended up in one Land of the Dead or another. Warriors who fell in battle were indeed selected to join Odin in Valhalla, where they spent their days fighting one another and committing deeds of great valor, and their nights feasting and drinking. It was believed that Odin gathered these brave warriors around him, not merely as a reward for their bravery and sacrifice, but also so that they could fight alongside him at Ragnarok, a battle during which Odin and his warriors were all doomed to die. It was, however, not exclusively those who died in battle who were welcomed into the halls of Valhalla, but any great warrior or leader who would be useful to Odin at Ragnarok.

The goddess Freya also welcomed the dead to her hall, known as Folkvang, the Field of the People. Unfortunately, very little information exists about Folkvang or who might be chosen to reside there. And of course, Vikings who died at sea might find themselves as guests in the underwater world of Aegir and Ran. The most common Land of the Dead, however, was Hel, an underground world presided over by a goddess of the same name. This was not a place of eternal damnation or torment, like the Christian concept of Hell, but rather a continuation of life in a new place. In Hel, the Vikings believed one would eat, drink, fight, and do all the things that they had done while they were alive.

Until the rise of Christianity, most Vikings believed in and worshiped many Norse gods and deities. They had no churches, temples, or religious buildings, and honored their gods in many different ways. Some of the symbols they used to represent their gods and beliefs can be found carved on rune stones, swords, axes, and other items that have survived from the Viking Age. One such powerful symbol that was displayed by many Vikings was Thor's hammer, Mjolnir. Carvings of Mjolnir can be found on weapons, boats, and Viking jewelry. Many Viking warriors wore a metal medallion of Thor's hammer as a necklace, in the same way that a Christian would wear a cross.

Since the Vikings were accustomed to worshiping many gods, they easily accepted the Christian god alongside their own. And in countries where they settled, like Normandy, Ireland, and throughout the British Isles, they quickly adopted Christianity. The exact reasons for this are unknown. But as mentioned earlier, trade played a role in the Viking conversion as Christians were not really supposed to trade with pagans. Although a full conversion does not seem to have been demanded of all Scandinavian traders, the custom of "primsigning" (first-signing) was introduced. This was a halfway step, falling short of baptism, but indicating some willingness to accept Christianity, and this was often deemed to be enough to allow trading. It also appears to have been due to political expediency for the Vikings to convert in order to form alliances or sign peace treaties. An example of this is the Treaty of Wedmore signed in 878. The treaty bound the Viking leader Guthrum to accept Christianity, with Alfred of Wessex as his godfather, and Alfred in turn recognized Guthrum as the ruler of East Anglia.[1] Whatever the Vikings reasons for converting at the time, the result was that by the end of the Viking Age, most of Scandinavia had converted to Christianity and the Norse pagan religion had been relegated to the realm of myths and legends.

[1] http://www.bbc.co.uk/history/ancient/vikings/religion_01.shtml

Conclusion

During the Viking Age, the Norsemen traveled far and wide. They raided, plundered, conquered, and settled throughout Europe, and their influence on the world can still be felt today.

These were the men and women who used their knowledge of the sea and navigation techniques to sail as far as the North American continent, five hundred years before Christopher Columbus. They used their shipbuilding skills to build swift, shallow-hulled dragon boats, the likes of which had never been seen before, to travel up rivers and raid and plunder far inland. They amassed mighty armies and used their prowess as warriors to conquer large parts of Europe and accumulate great wealth.

Men like Ragnar Lothbrok, Ivar the Boneless, Eric Bloodaxe, Egil Skallagrimsson, Erik the Red, and Leif Erikson, amongst others, all influenced history and changed the world they lived in. And while they were, for the most part, real people, they are also representative of their culture. The names of the common Vikings may have been long forgotten, but their bravery and spirit of adventure lives on in the stories and legends of these great men.

The Vikings had a profound influence on world history during the Viking Age, spreading their culture far and wide. They redefined the borders of the world they lived in and left their mark throughout Europe. Popular culture may predominately portray them as mighty warriors, raiders, and plunderers, but they were also settlers and explorers who exposed the world to Norse culture.

Legends and myths about the Vikings abound, and while they might not always be historically accurate, these stories have kept the memory of the Vikings alive in popular imagination and have made their history appealing to a large number of people, enabling the legacy of the Vikings to survive long after the end of the Viking Age.

Here's another Captivating History book we think you'd be interested in

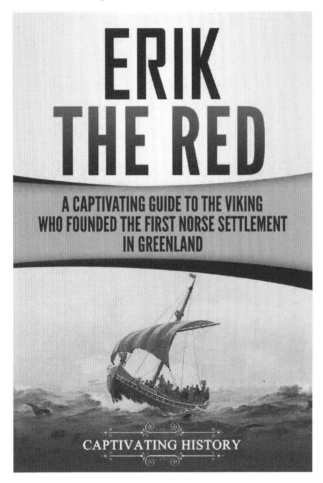

And another one…

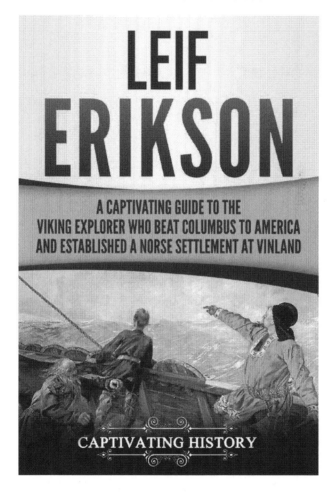

Free Bonus from Captivating History (Available for a Limited time)

Hi History Lovers!

Now you have a chance to join our exclusive history list so you can get your first history ebook for free as well as discounts and a potential to get more history books for free! Simply visit the link below to join.

Captivatinghistory.com/ebook

Also, make sure to follow us on:

Twitter: @Captivhistory

Facebook: Captivating History:@captivatinghistory

References

Websites

https://www.ancient-origins.net/viking

www.bbc.com/history/historic_figures/erikson.leif

http://www.bbc.co.uk/history/ancient/vikings/religion_01.shtml

www.britannica.com/biography/Leif.Eriksson-the-lucky

https://www.britannica.com/biography/Erik-the-Red

https://www.britannica.com/place/Vinland

https://www.britannica.com/technology/clinker-construction

www.biography.com/people/leif-eriksson

www.canadiannmysteries.ca

https://www.encyclopedia.com/people/history/explorers-travelers-and-conquerors-biographies/eric-red#1E1EricRed

http://www.englishmonarchs.co.uk/vikings.htm

http://hallucinations.enacademic.com/856/Hillingar_effect

https://history.howstuffworks.com/historical-figures/viking.htm

https://history.howstuffworks.com/historical-figures/viking1.htm

https://history.howstuffworks.com/historical-figures/viking2.htm

https://www.historyextra.com/period/viking/a-brief-history-of-the-vikings/

http://historylearning.com/medieval-england/harald-hardrada/

https://www.historyonthenet.com/viking-navigation-sailing-the-open-seas/

https://www.historyonthenet.com/the-viking-age-an-overview/

http://www.hurstwic.org/history/articles/mythology/religion/text/conversion_in_iceland.htm

https://inventorybag.com/blogs/normandescendants/historical-truth-of-ragnar-lodbrok

http://www.islandnet.com/~see/weather/elements/supmrge.htm

http://www.islandnet.com/~see/weather/history/artmirge.htm

www.leiferikson.org

http://mentalfloss.com/article/87312/7-myths-about-vikings-debunked

http://mentalfloss.com/article/78058/researchers-may-have-found-north-americas-second-viking-site

https://en.natmus.dk/historical-knowledge/denmark/prehistoric-period-until-1050-ad/the-viking-age/

https://norse-mythology.org/cosmology/the-nine-worlds/helheim/

https://norse-mythology.org/cosmology/valhalla/

http://www.populationfun.com/greenland-population/

https://www.q-files.com/history/vikings/everyday-life-in-viking-times/

https://www.ranker.com/list/details-about-blood-eagle-torture-method/melissa-sartore

http://www.sciencemag.org/news/2018/04/viking-seafarers-may-have-navigated-legendary-crystals

https://thedailybeagle.net/2013/06/23/bjorn-ironside-the-viking-ideal/

https://www.thevintagenews.com/2018/03/22/sweyn-forkbeard/

www.viking.no

http://vikings.wikia.com/wiki/Viking

https://en.wikipedia.org/wiki/Vikings

http://www.worldometers.info/world-population/greenland-population/

https://en.wikipedia.org/wiki/Greenland

Books and Articles

Danver, Steven (2010); Popular Controversies in World History: Investigating History's Intriguing Questions

A.M. Reeves et al; The Norse Discovery of America

The Icelandic Saga Database: The Saga of Erik the Red (sagadb.org/eiriks_saga_rauda.en.pdf)

Groenlendiga Saga (notendur.hi.is/haukurth/utgafa/Greenlanders.html)

D.J. Williamson et al; The Rules of Revenge; Viking Justice (All About History, Issue 059)

Davis, Graeme; The Cult of Thor (All About History, Issue 057)

Made in United States
Troutdale, OR
09/09/2023

12769728R00066